THIS JAPANESE LIFE.

ERYK SALVAGGIO.

For Keiko.

CONTENTS.

1.

ON PACKING A SUITCASE

FOR JAPAN.

First you will compress your entire life into two checked bags, 50 lbs and 62 inches each, and one sized 40 lbs and 42 inches. Measuring the (A) width, (B) height and (C) depth of the suitcase will give you the "size" of the suitcase:

A + B + C = SUITCASE

The airline offers no packing support hotline with bored operators reading scripts about how to competently eliminate everything that reminds you of your identity.

Nostalgia is heavy. I left my favorite books on my parents' shelves to make room for American toothpaste, with its fizzy fluorides, and a year's supply of Old Spice.

Here's what I took to Japan:

CONTENTS OF SUITCASE:

1 very nice suit (for meetings) It was a black suit and pants combination with a black tie. This was traditional funeral attire. I lost weight within six months of arriving that made it useless.

2 mediocre suit coats (for daily teaching)

2 ties (it's all I own)

5 Khaki pants (for daily teaching)

7 button-down shirts (for daily teaching)

7 T-shirts (for daily living)

Raincoat (Recommended)

3 pairs of shoes
One for work, one for going out, one for
dress. I would eventually pick up another
pair for running, but I didn't know I was a
runner when I packed.

30 pairs of socks

(Everyone will be looking at your socks. They
will point and be embarrassed for you if they
are dirty. You will buy more socks than you
can dream of ever buying.)

Swim Trunks, 1 pullover sweater

Layers for cold are better to pack than big,
bulky winter jackets.

For the classroom: 3 entry-level English-
language books, 30 small maps of my
hometown, 3 Sticker sheets.

Personal: 3 Cameras , 40+ Rolls of Film ,
Laptop, 1 copy of Essential Haiku by Robert
Hass, 1 copy of Franny and Zooey by JD
Salinger, 1 copy of Empire of Signs by Roland
Barthes, 3 Japanese-language books:
Learning the Kanji, 501 Japanese Verbs, J<-
>E Dictionary.

2.

ON GIVING UP EVERYTHING THAT WASN'T LISTED IN CHAPTER ONE AND FLYING TO JAPAN.

Somewhere over the Russian sea of Okhotsk, I am watching TV Champion: Naughty Puppy Trainers while listening to The Stone Roses singing "I Wanna Be Adored."

The in-flight navigation system tells me that the sun has set on my point of origin. It's nighttime in New England, it's 10 A.M. in Tokyo, tomorrow. My body is in all places at once. Exhausted and euphoric, like I've been awake all night, sleeping.

I have not slept. When I do, I hallucinate the chattering birds outside my bedroom window in Maine, the ones I'd wake up cursing. They do it again, not from the wing of the plane but from inside of my head.

With an hour to go before landing, the birds were replaced by a chirping female American tourist. Every sentence is a correction: "No, no, it's _____."

I'm sure I've made a mistake with my life. I stare out the window, miss my girlfriend, miss Montreal-style bagels with Hungarian cream cheese and coffee. I think of friends I will not see for two more years – and when I see them, we will not be the people we were when I was sitting on the plane. I knew it. My head tensed itself to fight tears.

"No, no, it's pronounced Shin-JAH-ka-yoo."

If you're afraid of flying, as I am, the best tactic is the one I use for fighting sadness. If a flight – or the time you face away from home – is overwhelming, let it be overwhelming when it is overwhelming. Don't anticipate fear or sadness. It will come, and when it does come, let it come, let it wash over you, then through you, and then go.

3.
ON INSECTS IN JAPAN.

There's a dead cicada on my porch, one of the swarm of hummingbird-sized insects that came out of their hibernation to welcome me to Fukuoka. They're loud, and while the guy hanging out upside-down on my foyer is cool, I stare at the living ones, wide-eyed with fears of what they'd do to my eyes.

The Cicadas (Semi in Japanese) have no mouths, but even that cannot stop the terrible rattling sound they make as the sun rises. They stop in the rain, but the rain is so loud that it doesn't matter. I'm up at 6 a.m. every morning because the semi are like roosters. There is also a rooster.

There is not an Internet connection, a television, or furniture. There are only dead cicadas. Sitting in my metal folding chair, sweating naked by the window, I stare at a dead cicada and listen to The Smiths.

This goes on for several days. My school is on vacation, but I must work anyway. I sit alone in an office with a supervisor who doesn't speak English, but occasionally buys me ice cream.

I come home and sit alone in an apartment to imagine craft projects for cicada corpses. I think of how to make tiny top hats, canes and monocles. I serenade the semi with my best Morrissey impression: "Cicada in a top hat, I know, I know, it's pretty serious."

Every day at 6 p.m., there's a chime and an announcement in Japanese, telling all the primary school kids to go home. Then, cicadas.

I walk up a hill outside my house to stone stairs that stop abruptly on a platform covered with wild grass. There's an abandoned playground to the side; an owl wind chime and more stairs, which lead to an old path in the forest and then, deeper in, a stone turned tall, written with a 1,000-year inscription in Kanji that I can't read and which (for that reason alone) must contain wisdom. Everything here is like The Legend of Zelda.

That day, thunder was rumbling near the city. Close by, the desperate chirping of dwindling and horny cicadas, the rustling of wind through trees, chanting monks, the further crowds of men cheering a baseball game, the digital beeps of the railroad crossing.

Nature in Japan is primal and overwhelming. It is everywhere. It pushes up stones on the sidewalk. When it rains, it floods canals, shooting straight up out of cracks in the sidewalk drains.

An old stone was up there, clearly once worth something, now crowded by weeds. So often, the ruins of public spaces are left to be overrun by nature in this ancient country. You can watch things being forgotten. Nature is pushing forward: Suburban sprawl interrupted by lush forest, crows stealing my laundry, apartments invaded by centipedes.

Everything sacred here shows awareness of its age and fate, what Lafcadio Hearn described in 1895:

"Buddhism taught that nature was a dream, an illusion, a phantasmagoria; but it also taught men how to seize the fleeting impressions of that dream, and how to interpret them in relation to the highest truth. And they learned well. In the flushed splendor of the blossom-bursts of spring, in the coming and the going of the cicadae, in the dying crimson of autumn foliage, in the ghostly beauty of snow, in the delusive motion of wave or cloud, they saw old parables of perpetual meaning. Even their calamities — fire, flood, earthquake, pestilence — interpreted to them unceasingly the doctrine of the eternal Vanishing."

The old shrine being swallowed by weeds makes me think about dead cicadas.

Americans fight death with plastic surgery and historic registers. Nothing collapses easily. But maybe exposing something precious to the air, unprotected, is a way of honing it to its true nature. The way that things age is uniquely and exquisitely theirs.

When I get back to the dead cicada, it's gone.

Eaten by a bird, perhaps, or tap dancing its way to heaven. I sit down on my folding chair and I wait for nature and Japan to do whatever nature and Japan will do.

4.
ON BOWING.

On the first day in the office I met an intern I had mistaken for a teacher. I had taken a default position of addressing everyone with safe formalities and bowing at an angle just short of tying my shoes.

The intern returned a deeper bow and I bowed in return, which he returned even deeper. This action recycled itself until the intern literally ran from the bowing radius. I'd find out later that the poor guy was bound by tradition to bow deeper than me.

Once I was told that I had to attend a practice assembly.

"It will be important for you to know when to stand up and sit down," they explained. Which is what we practiced for an hour and a half.

"Kiritsu!" (Stand.)
"Bei!" (Bow).
"Chokuseki!" (Sit).

For a half an hour, we did this; then the kids practiced singing their graduation song for a half hour. Then the practiced standing when their name was called for a half an hour.

I've learned a lot about bowing in Japan.

THE BOW.

Through observation, trial and error, I've discovered three types of bows.

1. **The Head Nod.** This is the casual bow you give when passing a peer or co-worker in the hallway or giving a stranger in your neighborhood a friendly "konbawa." You tip your head and maybe lean forward a little. You can also use this to make other foreigners look at their cell phones.

2. **The Slider.** This one is on a sliding scale from about 15 degrees to a full-blown, shoe-tying 45 degrees. The bend comes at the hip with your hands in front of your pants pockets (for men) or in front of your belt buckle (for women). Keep your eyes down when bowing. Adjust the depth of the bow and the duration for each situation, with a minimum of about 1 second. The 20-degree version of this bow is the most common.

3. **The Betraying Samurai.** This involves sitting on the ground with your legs folded like a half-assed push-up and touching the ground with your forehead. If you think you need to do this one, ask yourself: "Am I being deported?" If the answer is no, you can probably use a deep bow #2.

UNDERSTANDING THE BOW.

It seems like everything is broken down into smaller parts. Each part is given a beginning burst of energy, and the next piece is a new start. Bowing marks the beginning and end of any social interaction that isn't completely casual. You bow to mark the opening of a conversation, your partner bows to accept, and then you talk.

The equivalent in American English is the expression, "So..." You can gauge the degree of inconvenience or awkwardness someone is about to create by how many "o"s come after their "s."

Compare:

15 degrees: "So, do you wanna grab a beer tonight? My treat."

45 degrees: "Sooooooooooo, are you, uhh, planning on moving out of the house so I can move in with your ex-wife?"

Just imagine that every "o" is a half-inch further down, and you can figure out what kind of damage the bow is announcing.

When I leave work for the day, I bow to my supervisor in a jerky chicken-head-bob maneuver that is only accepted because I'm American. The proper bow would be 30 degrees, held for one second.

The remorse bow comes before a formal apology, and the depth and length of time depends on the offense. For egregious crimes you bow from the waist to form a 45-degree angle with your body. Police will often ask the instigator of a physical altercation to do this bow in lieu of arrest.

But perhaps you haven't started a knife-fight

at a bar or killed someone with drunken archery. Perhaps you just have to leave work early. For that kind of offense, you just cut the degree and duration of the bow. On the "So" scale:

15 degrees: "So, I'm sorry, but I have to go home and put out a fire."

45 degrees: "Soooooooo, I'm really sorry, but you have to go home, because I just set your house on fire."

During formal ceremonies the bow marks the beginning and end of each part of the event. When a new manager is hired, the new manager may come to the stage and bow. They'll be introduced, then bow and leave the stage. From there, they will instantly turn around, take to the stage and bow again before addressing the remaining business – say, a budget report. Bowing divides the two parts of the meeting: The first bow introduces the new manager, the second bow ends the introduction. The third bow announces the start of the budget report segment of the meeting.

To introduce the new manager and then have them go straight into the budget report would be pretty standard business in the US, but not in Japan. You want a clean and formal introduction, then you want it to shift to the full attention of the budget report.

Finally, there's the bow of a perpetually subservient class of the retail workers. Retail workers address you with a level of formality just below Emperor; the more enthusiastic clerks bow deeper in proportion to your bow, and they do it until they can't see you. A friend returned some defective merchandise at an electronics shop and was sent off by every employee in the store bowing at the doorway until he couldn't see them anymore.

You can always ignore retail bowing. If you are too egalitarian to let a bow go unanswered, think of it this way: they have to bow again, deeper, so by being "rude" you are actually preventing back injuries. Just say "sayonara" and call it a day.

5.
ON PSYCHIC SALARYMEN.

The first thing I did at my new job in Japan was sit at a desk for weeks without instructions. I'd eat lunch around 12:30, then sit at my desk. The vice principal of my school sat across the very long room. He didn't speak English but smiled enthusiastically when I entered and left. Once, he bought me ice cream.

My supervisor, Mr. Tanagawa, came in sometimes to ask if everything was going OK.

"I don't have anything to do, really."

"It's OK," Mr. Tanagawa said, "Don't try to do everything at once. Please relax."

I'd read English textbooks at my desk. Then I'd stare out the window, unsure if I was allowed to go outside. A teacher came in once, a teacher who spoke some English. I asked her if I could have a tour of the school.

"I'm sorry," she said. "No."

One day I came to work and there was a note on my desk with a single sentence: "There will be no electricity today." I sat in the dark with the vice principal as he read through an enormous stack of spontaneously generated paperwork.

Slowly teachers returned, and desks started to fill. An enormous Japanese man with a goatee came into my office with a tracksuit once. He went to the corner and started swinging a wooden stick around for 20 minutes. No one said anything about it. He left, and I didn't see him again for about a week, when all of the teachers came back. I was asked to prepare a 40-point listening test for students I hadn't met for a class I hadn't taught from a book I hadn't seen. It was due in a day.

That night, Mr. Tanagawa invited me for a "men's night out" with three high school teachers, for "locker-room talk." Only Mr. Tanagawa spoke proper English, but another teacher only spoke in English movie titles. He asked if I had tried a Japanese soup by pointing and asking, "First Contact?" I ordered salmon onigiri and he said I had a beautiful mind.

Despite the fun night out, nobody ever told me what to do. That continued for three years, and I've concluded that Japanese people are capable of psychic communication and expect the same of you. The Japanese mind-reading hypothesis will be controversial, so let me clarify:

1.   The school system in Japan controls every moment of a student's life. Rituals like standing and speaking in unison are practiced every hour. Lunch is eaten together. Uniforms and haircuts are regulated. Exceptions are rare. High school students spend the entire day with the same 40 kids for three years.

2.   Children are raised to speak carefully.

In America, that means using precise words and persuasive arguments. In Japan, it means vague, inoffensive chatter. Rather than argue, people kind of just hang out until they find common ground.

3. Under Japanese law, offending a samurai was punishable by instant execution, usually by being cut in half by the samurai's sword. This law lasted until 1873. For reference, that's when blue jeans were invented. I am not suggesting that fear of samurai has encouraged this behavior in the modern era, but if a country does stuff a certain way for a few centuries, those habits can linger.

A Japanese manager explained his culture's communication style to an American: "We are a homogeneous people and don't have to speak as much as you do here. When we say one word, we understand ten, but here you have to say ten to understand one."

I get it. In America I could pick up on the rhythm of people's lives. I could always tell if my roommate had gone to the grocery store or if my girlfriend had eaten dinner. But here, the rhythm was subtler, quieter. I was losing its tempo.

Instead of words and notes, there was body language, silences and facial expressions. The intake of air through the teeth with a cocked head means "no," the disconcerting slacker jaw-drop means "I see," which means "Yes." Learn these and you have a pretty comprehensive toolbox for Japanese communication. With some practice in my office, I'd learned to tell which kind of silence was positive and which was negative. It never stopped being really weird.

Nonetheless, I would be teaching a class called "Oral Communication."

6.
ON TEACHING ENGLISH
IN JAPAN.

Language lives inside our skulls, but only escapes through the tongue, that chunk of flesh pushing ideas out from our squishy insides to appease a primal urge to exude ourselves.

We are known by the sounds we make with our mouths. Standing in front of a classroom of bleary-eyed Japanese high school kids reading numbers for 50 minutes is a disorienting existentialist threat, like staring at a mirror while repeating your name.

In the classroom, language – my language, my "native tongue" – isn't a vessel that carries complicated, deep thoughts. The cargo I deliver here is not the secret understanding of German poets.

No. Today is phone number day. I will instruct the students on how phone numbers sound in America, a topic I never cared about:

The first three digits are read as single numbers, as are the following three: four-oh-three, two-seven-one. The last four are doubled up as pairs: "Forty-one-seventeen."

This is not true, but I was desperate to provide information rather than merely making noises.

Do this enough and you change.

In the real world, words cut up the environment. They change things, accomplish goals, order a cup of coffee. Words plant themselves in other people's ears and for a minute, you grow a little forest of meaning that you can both live in or argue about. In Japanese, the word for I, *watashi*, translates literally as "my part of our shared space."

Teaching English in Japan feels like planting seeds in concrete. Consider carrying on a conversation only to realize that it is, literally, a memorized from the textbook. Proper words get stripped of any connection to real meanings:

Student: "Hello!"
Me: "Hello!"
Student: "Thank you for asking!" (bright smile and a wave).

Of course, some students communicate something of their inner lives in English. I'm happy when they can tell me about their favorite bands or ask me what movies I've seen. They talk about food because we can all understand what food is. I am thrilled whenever words connect what's trapped inside two skulls.

"Eryk, this is frog?"
(She draws a terrible frog drawing).
"Uhm, maybe. Or a mouse?"
"Don't like frog."
(She crosses out the frog).

(I draw a frog).
"This is a frog."
"OK," she nods. "I like."

Sometimes I move to the back of the room and try to look at what I wrote on the board as if I can't understand it. It's almost impossible to forget that "four" means "four." But teaching with empathy means stopping yourself from knowing. You are outside of the black board and your inner monologue, thinking about sounds and pencil marks, and then you disappear for a second.

All those inexplicable Japanese T-shirts, those billboards that don't make any sense, happen because the English language doesn't refer to anything in Japan. It's a series of scripts and vocabulary words that produce test scores, not meaning. As a teacher, it's tempting to think that I am a real thing – that the students, someday, will actually speak to *me*. But I am not in the classroom. I'm a guy making noises that students repeat so they can repeat them later to another English speaker.

Even when things are understood, it doesn't mean they're clear.

7.
ON BOWLING IN JAPAN.

If you don't play a sport, you've run out of possible conversations with about 90 percent of Japanese men. So I started lying: "I'm a bowler."

At first it was a genius move. I was never asked to talk about the careers of obscure Japanese baseball players. I wouldn't have to explain the rules of "American Football." I'd just say I bowled.

Talk to one person as a new foreigner and watch what happens. My Japanese persona was quickly settled: I was a very passionate bowler.

It's not that I set out to lie. It started from a desperate, well-intentioned attempt to talk about something cross-cultural that wasn't food, sports, or Michael Jackson.

I had no recollection of my average bowling score. Very passionate bowlers ought to know this stuff. I made one up. Since the highest possible score was 360, I reasoned, I should place the number just above mediocre. "210," I said. The highest possible score is 300. My highest score was 120.

When the number impressed people, I realized I'd moved from polite white lies to outright boasting. I felt like a college freshman being awkward about my high school popularity.

"Ah, yeah, but it's a different scoring system," I'd tell them. "It's based on, uh, 360 points."

I blame Worcester, Mass., and New England's eccentric embrace of Candlepin Bowling over 10-Pin. This is already difficult for other Americans, but Candlepin uses balls slightly larger than a softball to hit narrow pins shaped like candlesticks. It's only played in Massachusetts, New Hampshire and Maine.

I had to research this to explain the game, which reinforced the opinion amongst my coworkers that I was very passionate about bowling. I was asked to teach a 50-minute class about Candlepin bowling with five minutes notice. I was given five minutes to transform hazy recollections about how bowling worked into a 50-minute class on American culture; an anthropologist submitting dreams as research.

Candlepin bowling was invented in the late 19th Century in Worcester, Mass., and the rest of the history is generally disputed. Nonetheless, the lesson included a great overview of German, French and Dutch settlements in the late 18th Century, and how anti-English settlement in the original colonies inspired Americans to invent a new kind of bowling just as they had envisioned a new destiny for the spirit of all men.

The rules for Candlepin bowling were impossible to explain in simple English, and I couldn't say "I don't know" to any question without unraveling the entire month-long web of deceit, which meant I'd be outed as a liar and forced to research obscure minor-league Japanese baseball players again.

They'd ask: How was the largest score 360 if there were 10 pins and 10 rounds? "Oh, did I say 10 pins? There are 12." How many times can you roll the ball? "Three times, but if you get them all down on the first try, you get to bowl two more times on your next turn and double the total from that score." Wouldn't that make the highest total 72 points, meaning the top score would be 866?

"Ah, yes, I guess it would." Blank stares. People stopped talking to me about bowling for a while.

Two months later I accepted an invitation to a school bowling tournament.

For two weeks, members from the other teams hovered around my desk. They'd ask a question they didn't need answered, then quickly launch an interrogation into my bowling skills.

"You're very passionate about bowling, aren't you, sensei?" I assumed it was small talk until bowling day arrived.

The bowling alley is identical to American Bowling alleys. Japan imports its bowling equipment along with the rainbow-colored lines painted on the walls behind multicolored silhouettes of bowlers.

America and Japan both had bowling heydays in the '70s and '80s, which is why so many bowling alleys look like Pac-Man museums.

The bowling was a little more intense than I expected. People had their own balls. Some had gloves. They were stretching. I asked one of the teachers if he bowled often.

"For this tournament," he told me, "I have come to practice for five days this week."

Japanese people can get excited about their hobbies, given the culture's embrace of give-it-your-all efforts and dismissal of anything less than 100 percent as laziness. You can do anything you want in Japan, except two things.

I bowled 110 in the first round. It was exactly my average and far below the inflated expectations of my politely agitated teammates. Everywhere around me, people were getting strikes and spares. I was hitting 6-8 pins.

"You are too nervous," they said. "You must relax."

Japanese sports are extensions of Japan's crafts. Craftsmen treat every part of the item as crucial. It's broken down into parts, isolated, and refined. Consider Kyudo, Japanese Archery. People train for months to practice mindful walking. Every step is conscious.

"To the sincere practitioner Kyudo is a way of life, and there is no separation between Kyudo training and everyday activities. Each arrow is shot as if it were the only one, just as each moment of one's life is the ultimate moment. The Kyudo practitioner does not look at the target for the result of his/her practice, but inward, for the target is not a target – it is a mirror. And if the heart is right, each shot clears away some more of the obstacles clouding the vision of one's true nature." - *Kyudo: Standing Zen*

I always did have a zen mind for bowling. With the ball in my hands, I'd look at the pins and decide what my body had to do to close the gap. Breathe, visualize, decide to act, and then act. It's not knocking down pins, it's rolling the ball with perfect form, which means perfect awareness, which means mindfulness and the discipline to keep it when the game starts to get dull.

Isolating these parts is the practice of mindfulness. Yes, it's in Japanese bowling strategies. It's also in television shows, paperwork and gas station attendants. For foreigners who see "mindfulness" as a mystical state instead of a cultural expectation it might be tempting to see a spiritual element within the strikes and the spares.

This isn't metaphysics. It's not spiritual. It's just the way other people do stuff. After all, my American approach to bowling is also cultural: Americans are efficient and easily bored. We're dilettantes and dabblers, people who join more than one club in high school, people who do many things well but rarely one thing perfectly.

I'm impatient. I rush things. I don't treat every new set of pins as a fresh challenge worthy of renewed focus. I had to relax, but didn't. I scored a 60 in the second round.

I went home that night and started reading up on Daisuke Matsuzaka.

8.
ON JAPANESE IMPROBABILITY.

"I think the students might be busy after school," said my new supervisor, Ms. Kuroguchi, "so perhaps they won't come to our meeting. I'm not sure. But if that's the case, we'll have to cancel the meeting for today."

In English, this sentence means that nobody knows what's going on yet, but we might cancel the meeting. In Japanese, it means that the teacher has spoken to the students, found out they have another appointment from exactly 3:55 to 4:35 p.m., verified the appointment and rescheduled the meeting. If we actually didn't know if the students were busy after school, I'd find that out through the same sentence.

Part of the problem with sharing the world with people is that eventually, you have to come to a consensus about it. Language usually gets the job done, but in a foreign tongue where I'm as eloquent as a trained raven, words are an unstable indicator of reality.

English is soaking with certainty. We teach assertion and self-confidence before we even teach how to formulate a compelling argument. The American ideal is to believe in yourself, and then you can do anything.

The Japanese language loves ambiguity.

Declarative sentences are arrogant. Nothing is spoken of as a permanent, factual thing. What they say, instead, is "*tabun*," which literally translates as "maybe" and expresses humble uncertainty over what Americans might call verified facts.

Most of the conversations I have with co-workers start with the words "probably," "maybe," or "perhaps." The threshold of uncertainty is pretty low. I may need a 60 percent chance or less to declare something "probable" rather than "certain," while in Japan the threshold hovers around 96 percent. "Probably" becomes anything between "definitely" and "never."

No one wants to hurt anyone's feelings by saying they're wrong, and one doesn't want their own feelings to get hurt by being wrong. This seems to be central to my Japanese life. Everyone – including yourself – needs space to back away from conflict. So we hedge: "Oh, I said it would *probably* happen." Because firm refusals or orders are taboo, Japanese culture can seem totally passive-aggressive. People drop a lot of hints.

"Ah, perhaps your co-workers are very busy, and will have extra work if you leave early today, ne?"

Sometimes this feels like entrapment. People don't ask for what they want. They build up to it, incrementally. It's a way of feeling things out, leaving space to adjust the plan or to imply negative news indirectly. For the English speakers unaccustomed to this indirect style – that is, those who haven't yet become psychic – it feels like we're slowly being pulled into a trap.

Ms. Kuroguchi asks, "Perhaps you have this Tuesday night free?"
"Yeah, I do."
"Maybe you can stay after school to meet with some students for a contest?"
"Oh, sure," I said.
"Maybe a half hour tomorrow?"
"Ah, OK, I can do that."
"But maybe there are three students," and the escalation begins – "So probably it will take an hour and a half. Sorry about that!"
"Oh, uhm, sure," I said, flustered. "An hour and a half tomorrow is fine."
"The contest is next month, so if you are free on Tuesday, perhaps they will want to meet with you each Tuesday. Is that alright?"
"Uhm, OK, so... you want me to meet with the students every Tuesday for an hour and half, for the entire month?"
"Oh, thank you so much, that will be very helpful."

I try to tell myself that I wasn't deliberately suckered into something. I was just being asked for a favor backwards. Probably.

After that, I thought I could just ignore the word altogether. But it's not enough to declare that the word "probably" means "certainly" when spoken in Japan, because "probably" also occasionally means "probably." Once, I was told that the bus for a field trip would "probably" leave at 9:30

a.m. I was wiser by then, so I kept my eye on the clock. At 9:15 a.m., a co-worker came up to chat, telling me I'd probably have a lot of free time today because of the field trip.

"Oh, I'm going on the field trip," I said, with foolish certainty.
"Ah. Perhaps you are going by car?"
"No, I'm taking the bus," I said. "I should probably get going?"
"Perhaps," the co-worker said. "But, I think, perhaps, the bus has already left?"
"I think it leaves at 9:30?" I said.
"Ah, maybe. But, I think perhaps it has already left."

Sure enough, it probably had.

9.
ON ROLLER SKATING.

Everything requires paperwork and stamped approvals. I had no idea what was on menus, how to do laundry, where they keep the cereal in grocery stores (the dessert aisle, it turns out). I wasn't sure when to bow, how to dodge bikes on the sidewalk, how to sign up for a mobile phone or access the Internet.

So I asked for help and I kept asking for hundreds of days, a constant unwanted burden on my supervisors and co-workers. I studied Japanese but seemed incapable of using it, trapped in the student's listening-practice dilemma of understanding 40 percent of what I heard while only expressing 10 percent of what I thought.

They moved Ms. Kuroguchi to the desk next to me. She would lean over and look at everything I was eating and ask me if foreigners could eat it.

I was constantly being offered help in areas where I was competent, or watched curiously as I tried to accomplish something new. The one thing I couldn't do was the one thing she asked me to do alone: When I filled out business trip forms in kanji, she would tell me the kanji was not drawn clearly enough, and to re-write the entire business trip form from scratch – a twenty minute process for me, a 3 minute process for her. I did it because I valued my independence.

Everyday, I was coming home and sitting in the bathtub. My girlfriend had moved to Japan a few months after I did and we'd shared an apartment. The arrangement would have been easy in America, but in Japan, I felt under siege: Stared at on buses and shopping malls, constantly corrected as I sat at my desk, questioned about why I wasn't studying Japanese more whenever I was studying Japanese. Students would linger around my neighborhood until 8 or 9 at night, always polite, but making a mental note of what I was doing and who I was with. In the bathtub, there was just me and the water, rising and falling as I inhaled and exhaled.

Culture shock goes deeper than being freaked out by robots at the mall or the high cost of apples. It's mild trauma, with phases that flow in and out over time. Your home culture is dead to you, your friends distant, the safety net of every certainty stripped away. Whenever someone spoke to me I'd panic, certain that I was about to endure another humiliating exchange, another chance to be helpless.

There are phases of culture shock:

The Honeymoon Phase, where the mall robot is cool and cute and weird and awesome and OMG JAPAN!!!!!

The Negotiation Phase, where you don't understand why you have to use a fucking robot to find out where the fucking shoe store is and you just KNOW the fucking shoe store isn't going to have your fucking size.

The Adjustment Phase, where you learn how to get the robot to work properly and you get that the robot is doing its best to help you out.

The Mastery Phase, where you don't even think about the robot as anything out of the ordinary.

I was living in phase two for months. Some people adapt, others don't. Either way, along the way to rejecting everything and heading home, or adopting the culture and staying forever, you're gonna get really effing cranky.

My first year Japanniversary coincided with an ambitious, two-week tour of Japan with my best friend from the States. As the Japanese speaker I was responsible for planning the itinerary, making reservations, sorting trains, communicating to taxi drivers and restaurant servers, asking for directions and finding vegetarian food in Japanese. I made mistakes. There were social ones, thanks to my Japanese cultural indoctrination ("Why are you apologizing for the rain?") and functional ones (I returned three times with the wrong ticket to the same station agent in a rural Kyushu train station. His annoyance was visible, and this is Japan).

You get kind of beat up. But then something happens. You're in the backseat of a taxi with a driver saying "ne" when he means "ka," but somehow you can tell he's warning you that the rope cars on the mountain you're planning to hike are closed. You're lost on the side of another mountain and some guy tells you where to go and somehow you understand him. My grammar was awful; I used weird particles and awkward constructions. My friend was impressed by the stream of Japanese escaping my mouth, but if the subtitles had been on she'd see I was saying, "Food, meat, no meat, OK? OK no meat food?"

Nonetheless, with natives in real situations, I stopped getting puzzled looks and started getting to the mountain, catching the right buses, ordering exactly what I wanted to eat.

The day after my friend left, I was feeling down. I snuck off to the roller skating rink. I wanted skates. I wanted dorky '50s drive-thru waitress gear, and I found them: Pink, Japan size 28, four wheels per shoe.

I totally expected to get out there and fall. I expected to get out there and be outperformed by 7-year-olds. I expected it to be a little like everything in Japan. But I remembered how to skate. It was instinctive. Shift weight from ankle to ankle. Twist a bit when you go around a curve. Lean a little to accelerate.

There were some hot shots on the floor and yeah, maybe some of them were 12-year-olds. But there was also an obstacle course of falling teenagers, middle-aged moms with no clue how to move and 20-year-old guys losing control and crashing into walls. But not me. I was moving. I was in control. And I was having fun.

Culture Shock comes in cycles.

10.
ON BEING SELFISH IN JAPAN.

I remember my high school French club. The kids smoked too young, wore black turtlenecks and talked about Camus, or more precisely, "spoke of Camus." The German club ate strudel, listened to polka and occasionally invaded the French club.

In America, alienated kids want to define themselves against the football/cheerleader standard. Whether you find it in *Nausea* or *Naruto*, foreign cultures feel personal and authentic, offering up a home abroad even when you're just living under a bloated stereotype.

I don't have an "American Club" in Japan. My Japanese English-Language Club does not sit around drinking Coke, reading The Great Gatsby or studying Bon Jovi lyrics. The kids do not want a "home abroad." Most of them never want to leave the city they live in.

So instead of watching Modern Family with a bucket of fried chicken, my club practices pronunciation and vocabulary. I've tried Harry Potter and Scrabble, but the other teacher – Ms. Kuroguchi – wouldn't tolerate that for very long. They needed to study for the University English entrance exams.

Every year the school has a festival where culture clubs and arts-oriented students show off a bunch of stuff they're doing – tea ceremonies, flower arrangements, origami, etc.

Akiko, a club member who, for the sake of my student confidentiality agreements, is also an ostrich, wanted to play the flute. She asked to skip some club sessions to practice, rather than spending five hours with us cutting construction paper. When the "situation" was brought to my attention, I shrugged and said "sure, whatever" without a second thought. But Japan doesn't understand "sure, whatever." Even "sure, whatever" requires a 20-minute business meeting and four stamps. Akiko's flute request unleashed a typhoon of righteous indignation: A committee of three teachers declared her selfish and demanded she quit the club, which she did, in tears. It was too late for me to intervene. I had already declared apathy and lost any influence I may have had.

Then, there's Kentaro. Ken plays – for the sake of my student confidentiality agreements – the keytar. Watching what happened to Akiko, and hoping to evade judgment from an ad hoc character evaluation committee, he quit the club before asking to play keytar for the culture show. Ms. Kuroguchi refused to speak to him. He, too, was "selfish." I was asked several times for my opinion on the matter. I finally shrugged and said: "I think there's a cultural difference."

An American might tell Kentaro or Akiko, "You have to do what makes you happy." I didn't say this to my co-workers because it would be incomprehensible. But as a psychic, Ms. Kuroguchi went on the defensive.

"What about the extra work the students would have to do if members skipped meetings?" They'd have to cut more paper while cracking jokes, I thought; I nodded.

"Just imagine how the other club members would feel."None of them care, I thought; I nodded.

"They didn't ask the club members first. They asked me first." Maybe they don't understand this weird process, I thought; I nodded.

Kentaro was not given permission to leave the club. He wanted to quit, so Ms. Kuroguchi didn't let him. I assumed this was a technicality, but he kept showing up and glancing, annoyed, at the ceiling.

"He has a sour face," Ms. Kuroguchi said. I nodded.

Americans are born American. We shoot out of the womb and start rolling around without a destination, and we do this until we're 30. We're encouraged to find *ourselves*, other babies be damned. If Americans are stones tumbled around until we find our inherent shape, the Japanese are chiseled to fit a precise mold. I suspect that Japanese kids come into high school as Americans and don't graduate until they're Japanese. The point of the school system – aside from teaching basic facts and training for jobs – is to chisel these kids into vessels for traditional Japanese values – to strip away the drive for self-definition at the expense of others, rather than cultivate it.

The reaction to even small transgressions in Japan can seem, to me, to be brutal and overwhelming. It's inspired by nature: Discipline in Japan comes with the force of a typhoon. Life is brutal, and that brutality keeps people in line by reminding them that they have to work together or everyone dies. If the kids forget this, teachers remind them by simulating a catastrophe. In America, we call it "being a dick."

You can see it in the lunch room. Eating lunch at a Junior High School in America was my first confrontation with the absurdity of life. It's an introduction to Lord-of-the-Flies social dynamics. The combination of half-formed brains, hormones, and the task of obtaining food purified the experience into Darwinism at its worst. You either developed a social strategy to survive, or you were consumed like the mystery meat doled out on our trays by rueful lunch ladies with bodies so ill-formed for such a gleefully malicious environment that one assumed they were secret masochists.

We quickly sorted into tribes of strengths or common weaknesses. I don't need to describe the cliques, it doesn't matter, none of us escaped without damage. Some of us got by on kindness. I learned to distract from any attention to myself by making jokes. It was a clumsy process with a lot of false starts. Lesser people resorted to withering insults, but I took the high road and stuck with puns, which made me ill-suited for any room younger than 55.

The pinnacle of my lunchtime Galapagos experiment was the outbreak of a war between factions of bullies. How it started is irrelevant, but the end result was two 14-year-old toughs circling each other wielding food products like pocket knives. In one hand, a hot dog doused in ketchup, in the other, a vanilla ice cream cone. The two circled each other, alternatively tossing out curse words or taking a stab at the other with the remnants of lunch. Neither was held with any degree of self-awareness, but at that point I, as an observer, was comforted by the sudden and unexpected realization that everything in my life was completely meaningless.

Contrast this with a lunchroom in Japan: The Japanese government – which does not value American individualism – steps in, encouraging students to thoughtfully reflect on their social behavior. To paraphrase a Japanese Education Minister, lunch is a part of education, not a break from it. Primary school "lunch lessons" teach students how to engage in proper lunchtime rituals, including socializing. While it might sound like Orwellian conditioning, others might see it merely as training on social manners and etiquette.

This regimented social training has its ups and downs. For one, relying on social protocols over social Darwinism teaches the kids how to perform at lunch – to eat food they don't like, make conversation with people they don't like, and express gratitude (and platitudes) whether they like it or not. How do you foster expression in a regimented way, since clumsily learning individual expression is precisely what makes American teenagers such assholes? You guide kids through respecting other people's space and responsibilities. We don't have that in America: We teach about freedom, then let kids practice their freedom at lunch. By contrast to Japan, that's America's idea of the fundamental reason humans live: To make ourselves happy first, and occasionally compromise with other people along the way, because occasionally compromising makes us good people.

Here, occasionally not compromising defines selfish people. A kid wants to play the flute in a music festival, and they end up tearfully apologizing to a room full of teachers. Witnessing these "lessons" can be disturbing. But I imagine what my high school would look like to my Japanese coworkers, terrified by the idea that "You have to do what makes you happy."

If "selfishness" is the unintended byproduct of liberty, Japan teaches selflessness without any respect for liberty. Preserving social cohesion and tradition are more important values.

11.
ON SNEEZING IN JAPAN.

In my first days in Japan, I'd ask, "What do you say in Japanese when people sneeze?" Occasionally I'd hear "odaiji ni" as an option. So I said "odaiji ni" to anyone I caught sneezing. In truth, no one says a word in response to an "atchoo!" (or "hakushun!"). Why would they? A sneeze is not a question. I'd asked the question, so people had to imagine an answer. But "Odaiji ni" is something between "get well soon" and "there but for the grace of God go I."

There's a word for a sneeze in Japan – *kushyami* – which matches the history of the English sneeze prayer. Just as we'd bless the sneezer to protect him from the evil spirit that may enter his body, the Japanese would name the sneeze.

An unnamed spirit within the sneeze could return and try to kill you. So people nearby would declare "you see death!" (as in, "That guy you just sneezed out, his name is death!") so that everyone knew a sneeze-spirit was hanging out.

If this sounds ridiculous, well, the Japanese have given it up. Like, a hundred thousand years ago. I'm American. From the cradle, I was surrounded by the English language, baths in the same room as toilets, and people who say "God Bless You" to a sneezing person. I would never consider that I could just say nothing. Which is a challenge of life abroad. How do you know what to do, when you don't even know you're supposed to do something?

"[T]here are known knowns; there are things we know we know. We also know there are known unknowns; that is to say we know there are some things we do not know. But there are also unknown unknowns – there are things we do not know we don't know." - US Secretary of Defense, Donald Rumsfeld.

As a foreigner in Japan, I am the counterpart to a Japanese visitor to America, constantly looking at a sneeze without recognizing it as a spiritual moment. There are known knowns: I know I need to bow and take my shoes off when I go inside. There are known unknowns: I know that I don't know how to behave at a Japanese wedding, or how to report that my bike has been stolen. For those things, I know enough to ask for help.

The unknown unknowns, of course, I can't list. I'm ignorant to an entire world of Japanese expectations. If a Japanese tourist standing next to you responds to your sneeze with awkward silence, he doesn't know he's expected to say something. And he doesn't know that he doesn't know. He doesn't think to ask, "What do I say when people sneeze?" because he doesn't imagine that he should have to say anything. It's not his world.

Working in Japan, I have expectations and obligations. I can't ask questions about these obligations if I don't know that they exist. I have to imagine all possible worlds, examine the consequences of my actions in each of those worlds, and then act.

I'm Schrodinger's Expat. In the thought experiment proposed by Austrian physicist Erwin Schrödinger in 1935, a cat is placed into a box with a radioactive substance and a device which, if it detects a split particle, releases a hammer on a vial of poison. Then you put a cat in the box and seal it. At any point in time, the hammer might drop and release the poison. (No, he didn't actually do this, though thousands of theoretical cats are killed by philosophy students every year).

The cat is inside the box and, presumably, the cat knows if she is still alive. But nobody outside of the box has the slightest idea. We've got a dead cat on our hands, or we don't. The universe has split into two separate paths. Some physicists argue that the cat is alive in one universe and dead in another. You just don't know which universe you live in until you open the box and see.

That's my life.

You never know when the stray atoms of a faux pas will trigger a vial of social poison to trigger a catastrophe. I would not know, for example, that when sending an e-mail in an office, one should order the names in the CC field by the order of their rank in the company and that failure to do so is an insult, which is actually the case in Japan.

Which takes us back to Schrodinger's cat: In a world where the cat is running around after you open the box, you don't ask questions about the world in which the cat is dead. When I break a rule, most people rack it up to being a wacky foreigner. But sometimes someone gets angry. "Why didn't you ASK how the names in the CC field should be organized?"

We are born with a basic set of operating instructions, passed on by past generations: Shit, eat, look around. That's all you did as a stupid kid. The core DNA kicked in a few more surprises at puberty and into old age. For most of it, though, we're on your own.

We have a lot of time for putting your hands through every carpet, our tiny fingers picking up lint and rocks and acorns and sticking them up our noses. Our parents love us in certain ways and so we decide to test that, and based on those tests we decide what love will be.

Every day starts as an unknown unknown. But then we start focusing on the known unknowns. We come up with a new set of experiments designed to do one thing: Get what you need to ask the next question. A child in the developing world, you might guess, has few opportunities to run his tiny fingers through the carpet, and so his sense of touch is shaped by grass and plaster instead of nylon or cotton and laundry machines. We are limited by the scope of our imaginations.

Your world narrows from childhood, and you may not always notice the colors of leaves or the weirdness of all the paperwork you're supposed to file. You move through the world, missing a lot, but doing a lot. Your childhood is spent whittling the possible into the practical, and then you're called an adult. Until you move to Japan.

So, how do you live in a culture where everything is an unknown unknown, where you never know the name of the sneeze? To roughly paraphrase the Copenhagen interpretation from quantum mechanics: You've got to screw up.

Niels Bohr solved the Schrodinger's Cat paradox by saying: Hey, the cat isn't dead or alive until it's observed. You have to open up the box and see if you killed the cat. Until you do, it's all just theory. Bohr is just like those ancient superstitious Japanese men naming the sneeze: If someone spews a bunch of particles everywhere, you'd better see it. You'd better point at it and call it out: "You are death!"

Likewise, I realized that to survive, I would occasionally be subjected to the angry Japanese coworkers who expected me to live by Japanese customs and philosophies, ideas they have a hard time imagining aren't universal. They, too, are limited by the scope of their imaginations. They can't imagine the scope of what I don't know.

I like to live by the maxim, "Be honest, be earnest, and hope the cat's still alive." One hopes no one is offended, demands your resignation or avoids you at parties when you take a risky action. But at least you'll know which world you're living in.

12.
ON ALWAYS HAVING AN EMPTY SEAT NEXT TO YOU IN JAPAN.

On a recent trip to the near-abandoned coal mining town of Tagawa, I took the wrong train three times, taking me into the true inaka – Japan's rural backwater.

The sight of a foreigner in these parts is rarer than where I live, which is a moderately cosmopolitan city of about 5 million. In one station, positioned to bring rice farmers to another, more far-away rice farm, I sat down with 15 minutes to spare before departure. People trickled in and formed a bubble around me. The seat at my side remained unoccupied until a Junior High School boy sat down, staring absentmindedly at a cell phone screen.

Realizing what he'd done, he leaned forward and nodded at the next guy, who slid over. The boy followed, and I was left with five inches of extra space on my right. This is the "Gaijin Forcefield," a foreigner's super power in which we are given extra space on public transportation to accommodate our enormous frames, even if those frames are the same size as a typical Japanese guy.

Among the expat bitterness brigade, this superpower is a go-to example of casual racism in Japan. Japan apologists say it is simply hospitality run amok, the generous Japanese spirit toward foreigners runneth over into giving Westerners the space that they are said to want.

The answer is somewhere between – it's just one example of the constant hum of "otherness" that buzzes around foreigners, a frequency always off-kilter from what I presume are the bright harmonics otherwise felt in a train car full of *Nihonjin*.

This isn't to dismiss actual racism against any group of people in Japan, whose real gripes include landlords refusing to rent apartments to foreigners, banks denying credit cards, police administering random inspections of ID cards or passports. I've heard stories of *inaka* school girls calling out the smelly foreigner to their friends.

This kind of direct racism has consequences beyond people feeling left out, and of course all of you are smart enough to know that this kind of racism is reserved for stupid people and the elderly.

Being a foreigner in Japan is inherently disruptive. It goes against Japanese etiquette, which emphasizes that you don't stand out or make people uncomfortable. Your existence shatters these ideals before you even open your mouth.

I am an unknown thing in Japan, a country with 99.8 percent ethnic homogeneity. People react to novelty in different ways. The idea that the Japanese should ignore my ethnic distinction is incredibly unrealistic. I may as well be a polar bear on a train, and it's impossible to expect people to treat a polar bear like an everyday occurrence, at least until polar bears start riding the subway with any degree of regularity, undoubtedly with better navigation skills than my own.

How we choose to internalize this "othering" is up to us. I see it as an opportunity to practice thoughtful behaviors instead of embracing instincts and gut feelings or declaring that, woe is me, someone on a train doesn't think I'm an amazing, wonderful person.

Since I know I am unlikely to force the Japanese into being accustomed to polar bears, I may as well adjust how I react to their reactions. When I start to imagine that there's hostility hiding behind some arbitrary actions, I remember high school.

If you went to a public American high school, you will understand what life is like as a foreigner in Japan. There is an in-crowd – the Japanese – and there is an out-crowd: You. Sure, there were the high school nerds, the less-than-88-percent-assimilated-ethnic-kids, band geeks, theater nerds, punks, etc. There were rivalries between those groups, but there was also a small group of kids who were simply ignored. They tended to join forces and quietly observe the nonsense going on around them, occasionally making jokes or pithy observations, but rarely stepping up to challenge anything because they were too detached to care. Perhaps detachment is the lingering symptom of an alienated smart kid in recovery.

Perhaps this kind of detachment is what leads a person to uproot and move in the first place. People who feel particularly drawn toward foreign places, those who trust their own tolerance to handle perpetual outsiderness, often have some training and that training, I'd bet, is the social space that occupies public schools in America.

Oddly, few of us seem to stop to acknowledge how much of our attitudes and beliefs about the world outside of us were rules written by our dumbass 16-year-old selves in reaction to a bunch of other dumbass 16-year-olds.

I'm comfortable with living as a passive and detached observer, which is why I'm comfortable, sometimes, as an illiterate foreigner in Japan. If you get detached enough, you start to see the active role you're playing in events because you are shaping the story of those events regardless of how you act.

I often have to remind myself that I am interpreting this culture through a paranoid lens – I'm being stared at, I'm being ignored when I say hello, I'm being talked about on trains. It's the realization of all fears for self-obsessed neurotics: In America, I comforted myself with the realization that, in fact, everyone is too busy thinking about themselves to notice anything I'm up to.

But in Japan, that just doesn't hold up. I actually am being stared at, inspected and judged.

So you decide how you're going to handle that. You can look at the five-inch-wide patch of blue cloth glued to the seat between you and the junior high school student on the train, and you can decide if it's racism or cultural accommodation, you can decide if he's uncomfortable with you or being polite, you can decide you smell bad or that he's worried that he smells bad.

You can ask him, you can ignore him, you can relax because you have the space, you can laugh because his ignorance has made for a more comfortable train ride, you can wonder if, maybe, just maybe, you actually DO smell bad.

But we'll actually never know. This mystery in the chasm between you and the consciousness of a boy in the sailor uniform is just as unknowable as the chasm between you and the consciousness of God. I can decide to dismiss all those perceived indignities I'm being forced to endure. Or I can sit there and make up a story, pretend that story is the world, and then go ahead and live in the world that I just invented, like a crazy person.

We have a choice. We don't really have to care what the 15-year-old sitting next to us, or inside of us, or running the entire universe thinks about us. We'll never really know, anyway.

13.
ON RAMEN HANGOVERS.

When someone assures me, with profound sincerity, that they don't have a drinking problem, I assume they have a sincerely profound drinking problem. Yes, as an expat in Japan I drink with greater frequency and to greater excess than I have at any other time in my life. But I assure you, with profound sincerity, that I don't have a drinking problem.

What I have is a Japan problem. If it weren't for cars, the nation's chief manufactured export would be bottles of self-expression extracted from the pent-up anxiety of Japanese office workers. Red-faced men cracking open a beer takes on the symbolic airs of a ritual: The crack and pour of a social release. There's emotion pouring out of that bottle.

Drinking parties are job requirements. Japan even has a product that lets you consume more alcohol while getting less drunk. Think about that for a minute: You pay 100 yen to consume more but feel it less. This only makes sense in a culture of competitive, shot-for-shot drinking, where keeping pace with your coworkers and superiors is rule *ichiban*.

According to one study:

"Sixty percent of problem drinkers are salaried businessmen who claim that getting drunk with clients or coworkers is part of their job and a mark of company loyalty. To refuse a drink from the boss is a terrible insult that can damage a career. And although alcohol consumption is now decreasing in most industrialized countries, it has quadrupled in Japan since 1960."

The typical Japanese person consumes 6.5 liters of alcohol per year. The typical Japanese person also contains about 6.5 liters of blood. This isn't exactly crazy, given that Korea, the United States, Canada and Great Britain all beat Japan in per capita drinking games. Japan is sixth in the world for beer consumption, under China, the U.S., Germany, Brazil and Russia. It's not that the Japanese drink more than any other country, it's that most of it seems to be consumed in single sessions.

There are a lot of good reasons to have a drinking problem in Japan. Here are 5 of them.

Brinksmanship

The Japanese are terrified of failure and that includes drinking games. The unspoken rules of the Japanese drinking game are as follows: Every time you see a co-worker at a work party, take a shot. If that co-worker is a superior, take two. You play this game at every single work party, or *enkai*, in Japan.

The etiquette of the enkai demands that you accept a drink when it's poured for you. To refuse the pour is to refuse the conversation about the pouring. Unless you have to drive, there's no reason to say no to a refill, and enormous social pressure to say yes. People will refill your drink regardless of how empty the glass is, and so you have to take a shot to make room for the new pour. It's just polite.

If you stop playing, the consequences are pretty real. In the States, we'd say you're a healthy, reasonable person that employers would want to hire and promote. In Japan, it shows a reluctance to trust your co-workers with inebriated openness. If you really liked us, you wouldn't worry about losing control.

Not drinking skips out on the shared joy of the night and the shared misery of the morning after. Many mandatory drinking parties aren't even scheduled on weekends – they're scheduled on Thursdays, with the idea being that on Friday, you'll all continue to cement the bond of the night before by working through a hangover. Together. It's a team-building exercise.

Nomunication
In Japan, openly discussing a problem is part of the problem. You're bound to spill into messy accusations or assumptions, someone's face will get lost and their day ruined. So people wait until they're drunk to say anything at all.

What's said while drunk is always forgiven, under the same don't-discuss-the-problem rules that created the problem in the first place.

The expat term for this is "nomunication," a portmanteau of "nomu," meaning "to drink" in Japanese, and "communication."

If you drink with co-workers, you'll start to hear people complain about other co-workers. This is the unsurprising result of the alcohol, but also an essential and anticipated aspect of the *enkai*: Blowing off steam and allowing a window of blunt, direct complaints to be noted and forgiven, with the "outbursts" forgiven by copious amounts of booze.

Other people will confide secrets about which co-worker they are in love with, what they think of so-and-so's English and that you work so hard they can't trust you. (I've been told all of these things). You may be asked who is the laziest co-worker. You may be asked to arm-wrestle.

In the morning, the harsh words (by Japanese standards) are remembered and, usually, corrected, without any further confrontation, while the drunken loudmouth is off the hook. Also, none of the secretly fluent friends from an *enkai* will acknowledge you again, until the next one.

Nomunication is actually one of the most effective ways to get an office conflict resolved in Japan. You drink with the person you don't like, until you are back-slapping familiar, then you say what pissed you off in a single sentence, then how sorry you are about mentioning it for the next ten. It's the Japanese version of the "I love you, man."

Loneliness

Japan is a country of introverts. Children are raised to cultivate reflection and present a very specific kind of face to others, regardless of their inner state. That face should be calm, collected, dignified and friendly, with very specific events that call for very specific exceptions.

People don't approach each other, and so you have people working side by side for hours a day (often more than 10) who don't know much about the other. Alcohol helps people ease quickly into personal interactions with little shame, the safety net of alcohol catching their many falls into social awkwardness.

This tends to be especially true of expats, usually young and otherwise unaccustomed to 12-hour workdays and Japanese rigidity. When and if the "weekend" comes, alcohol accelerates the descent into relaxation and "cutting loose." You skip right to a 2 a.m. feeling by 8 p.m. and, given how long a work day is, that leaves extra time to sleep.

Tolerance

There's no social stigma against alcohol in Japan. There was never a prohibition era, and Japanese drunks tend to stay polite up to and beyond vomiting on someone (and surprisingly, being vomited on). The consequences of drinking in the west – violence, drunk driving accidents, etc – are mitigated by Japanese restraint and an excellent public transportation network.

Drinking doesn't have a stigma, so restrictions on alcohol are pretty loose – at least to Americans – and so beer vending machines or train passengers holding open cans (though rare) quickly lose their shock value.

There's even a product called "Kid's Beer." It's basically carbonated apple cider, but I'm from a country that banned candy cigarettes.

Nomihodai
Bars, Karaoke booths, or restaurants offer up as much alcohol as you want for a set price and time, usually meaning about five or six drinks over two hours. "Binge drinking," according to the US Center for Disease Control and Prevention, is the consumption of five or more drinks in two hours. In other words, Japanese establishments are basically promoting binge-drinking specials. At one party, a tired wait staff simply handed over several pitchers of Gin and Tonics, rather than taking single drink orders.

For all this, Japan is surprisingly reluctant to the idea of alcoholism and treatment. Japanese researchers suggest that there are 2.4 million alcoholics in Japan, and that only 22,000 of them are seeking treatment.

The Japanese are more inclined to limit "alcoholism" to disruptions caused by drinking at inappropriate times, or violent or angry behavior (though not necessarily grabby-handed men). When that happens, it's not so much seen as a disease as a failure to control oneself.

Alcoholism as an addiction isn't an easy sell in Japan, where personal responsibility is everything. Treatment often comes down to scrubbing out the negative behaviors that come with drinking, rather than eliminating drinking altogether.

On a personal level, the best way to scrub out the effects of drinking is with a bowl of ramen.

Ramen is, hands down, the best food to eat when drunk and the worst food for the next day's hangover. In the midst of drinking, ramen shifts my brain's attention to fats and proteins, a pleasing distraction from the bubbling, hoppy mess of Asahi or Kirin beers swishing around in my stomach.

Two pints of beer is enough to unravel a brain's sense of appetite control. Scientists have proven as much – food looks better when you're drunk, your appetite is unbound.

You eat ramen, and then ramen is psychologically bonded to the alcohol like a baby duck looking at its mom. So the next time you drink, you'll crave the same thing – a high-calorie blend of fatty salts. The downside is that your appetite is not the only thing your body is losing control over. You urinate more – oh, the romance! – not because beer is any more "liquid" than water, but because you just can't hold it the way you would when you are sober. So you quickly become dehydrated, which adds to the headache and general unpleasantness of a hangover. The salt from ramen doesn't help.

No one really knows why people crave the worst foods we could eat when we're drunk. Most likely, bodies get confused while trying to pump a literal poison out of your system. The body needs energy to fight the toxic brew. Fat and sugars are the fastest way to get energy into your body in the short-term, but we end up spending that energy on late-night karaoke binges.

One thing I have learned at my lowest points in Japan: The body is often compelled towards precisely what it shouldn't have.

14.
ON BEING ALONE IN A ROOM
IN JAPAN.

I once saw a man staring at a handheld television set on a train, eyes swelling with tears, looking at what might have been video footage of a woman gazing back at him, her eyes wet with empathy and openness.

I wondered if Japan had a special market for DVDs of women sadly staring through the TV frame into the eyes of lonely salary men, distracting them from the complex horror of solitude.

It was just some sort of weird toothpaste commercial, the man perhaps had allergies.

***

The trouble with being alone in Japan isn't being alone in Japan – we are alone everywhere, born with nothing and lucky to have whatever we get. The trouble with being alone in Japan is that distracting myself requires more effort that I'd have to extend at home.

What I do, the central activity of my life in Japan, is spending time alone in a room.

You can identify the symptoms of being alone in a room for too long whenever you come across another expat, myself most certainly included. You know someone's been alone in a room for a while if: There's a struggle to keep up conversational monopolies, a tendency to over share, a willingness to indulge in bouts of emotional intensity while recoiling from the same display by others.

If my normal social life was a series of power lines connecting and delivering power in stable flows, my life in Japan is more like a series of sparking frayed wires jumping around a quiet road, desperate to electrocute passerby.

Curbing the intensity of that interaction means getting used to sitting alone in a room. This is Zen, which is great. Japan has a long history of sitting alone in rooms. But it's not like I can go to a temple and find some guy to draft up a map of the gnarled forest in my skull. More realistically, I'm going to sit alone in a room.

Conversations about loneliness tend to draw pity. This is a shame, because this blocks most constructive conversations about what it means to be alone. Time and place, and all that, but being alone isn't a confession and it is not the exclusive conversational domain of depressed people. It's a fact of life, particularly a life lived in a foreign country known for isolation and aloofness, a nation run by cats. It would be better and more sane for us to talk about this rather than not talk about it. It's a major part of the expat life.

Japan breeds a certain isolation already, with

traditions of shyness, long work hours, and reliance on peace and quiet. As a foreigner used to gregarious back-slapping and arbitrary conversations with strangers, this starts to feel extreme.

So I will sit alone in a room and feel frustrated by it. Zen tells us that the frustration is a delusion – tell yourself that, and let it go. There's a short moment of serenity when it starts to work, when I'm present, and then I think about the Internet.

The world in a photograph is saved for a while, but everything outside the photograph is over. You bring it back by thinking about it, a tempting bit of sorcery. It's why we tell stories about the things that happen. We get to bring them back, think of some meanings, and pass them on to other people. This is the source of pain and the solace from it, the good-cop/bad-cop relationship we have with life.

That's why sitting still in a room feels a lot like dying. I'm living in the space just outside the photograph. No one's seeing me. I'm not chasing novelty into a story to tell later. I'm sitting alone in a room, trying to be present and dealing with the idea that I'm losing time. When it's time to stop thinking about sitting alone in a room, I'll stop. I will want to talk to someone about it, but there won't be anyone to talk to about it. So perhaps I will run, or cook, or read, or watch TV.

I came to Japan precisely to face this kind of unhappiness, and take it on. I wanted to find the holes where my mental energy was leaking and paste them over with *kaitenzushi* and a caulk gun. I want to live apart from everything else, craving nothing, aloof and detached and in love with everything without expectations. I have yet to find some furnace in my chest that takes up self-doubt and burns it into some perfect crystal vision.

I think it's probably not gonna happen, and that's a relief. I can't be mindful all the time. Zen isn't about becoming a Buddhist Superman, and that self-imposed struggle can only remind me that I'm falling short.

***

Muho Noelke, a German-born abbot of the Antai-ji Zen temple, writes:

Don't be mindful, please! When you walk, just walk. Let the walk walk. Let the talk talk. Let the eating eat, the sitting sit, the work work. Let sleep sleep.

Novelty makes for a good story, an "interesting life," but it's not actually happening when you are sitting alone in a room, even if that room is in Japan, and that's why it's important to learn how to do it. I start to lose that story of who I am, that person I'm so fond of, that person who is eventually going to disappear unremembered, all that wasted time spent unobserved and unobservant. I'm scared of being the person outside of that metaphorical photograph. I cling to it. It's an ego thing. I don't want to disappear, I spent a lot of time making me.

So I sit and think, and invent problems to react to and analyze and make into stories – squeeze it back into the picture frame – to make life compelling enough to talk about later. But that's a kind of failure. My real success, the real Zen achievement, is sitting down, shutting up, and letting all that nothing happen without turning it into a story.

15.
ON BEING BORED.

"You're going to have the best time of your life."

I heard this a lot from people before I left. Nobody meant for it to stress me out. When we think about "the adventures of a lifetime," living abroad is at the top of the list. But how many nights did I go out based on subconscious compulsion to "have the best time of my life?" How much did this compound the feeling of failure and insecurity about my ability to cope in Japan?

Sometime during college I realized I was a workaholic. Without workahol, I devolved into a spectre surrounded with the fog of free-floating anxiety. My college days started at 7 a.m. and classes ended at 4 p.m.; I'd drive to the newspaper for the overnight copy editing shift and sleep at 2:30 in the morning.

On holidays, I would collapse from exhaustion, wake up at 5 in the afternoon and find that most of my friends had left the godforsaken Maine town we all lived in. I'd go to the bookstore, get a cup of coffee and read The Economist. In Japan on a laptop, I was an elf fighting dragons with a bow and arrow stolen from an orc.

My mother had sent a box of homemade Christmas cookies that had taken nine days to get to my apartment. The purple haze covering these cookies couldn't have been intended, but the safety of these 14-day-old sweets was an open question I was determined to answer. For one day I literally did nothing but eat questionable cookies and hunt groups of cat-faced bandits.

I wondered if all the personal growth I had experienced in Japan was an illusion, and that the last full evolution of my self took place when I was 15 years old. I was eating Twizzlers, drinking soda and trying to figure out if I should invest perk points into destruction or restoration magic.

The next day I decided to invest in the pursuits of a physically and psychologically healthy man. I would run, no matter how cold it was, if for no reason other than to dissolve my guilt over sitting on a couch drinking Cassius-flavored Holiday Ginger Ale.

On the way to the park I had my first interaction with another human being in nearly three days – an NPC, in gaming parlance – with the local udon shop owner as he straddled a scooter at a stoplight.

"Eriku-san, country? Coming back? Back, country?"
I made the "I don't understand" face. "Country, back? You come back." Then, sounding angry, "HOME COUNTRY!"

"I didn't go," I said. "Ikkimasen!"
"Oh. Oh. Oh. When? When... did... you...

go?"
"Tuesday," I said.
"Where, where where?"
"Hong Kong. I came back Tuesday. Tuesday. Hong Kong. Kara kimashita."
He asked about my ex-girlfriend.
"I don't know," I said.

I finished 5k and considered going for 10k, when my face got hit with a blast of wind and I went home. 23 hours and 14 minutes to go.

The day after New Year's Day is a national holiday, and so is the day after that. Japan's schools have three kinds of "days off." The holiday where teachers and students come in and have classes, the holiday where students stay home but teachers have to sleep in the staff room and the actual holiday, where nobody comes to school.

I walked to school, not knowing which of the "holidays" it was. Actually I wasn't sure what day of the week it was or when I had last shaved. I reflexively scanned the sky for signs of dragons. Work was an empty parking lot and a locked door. I took note of an inexplicably large poster advertising Mission Impossible 3: Ghost Protocol hanging in the hallway.

Walking home, I thought back to the conversation I'd had with Ms. Kuroguchi before I'd left for Hong Kong.

"So I'll come back on the third?" I asked.
"Oh, thank you so much, but the students may want to have a vacation," she said.

"Oh, I see. Well, I can come in on the third, and if any of the club members want to meet me for extra practice, I'll be in the office."

"Oh, thank you so much, but maybe there will be very few teachers here on that day," she replied. "Probably, I will take the day off to see my family. I'm so sorry!"

"I see, that's OK, just tell the students to find me if they want to meet."

"Oh, thank you so much! But maybe very few students will be here on that day."

***

That afternoon I was home alone, looking at people's pictures on Facebook. Everyone was smiling in the midst of some drunken romp, and I was asking myself, "Why am I not having as much fun? What's wrong with me?"

It seemed like everyone had come to Japan and thrived enough to smile at me through wall feeds, drunk and happy and *changed,* while nothing had changed about who I fundamentally was. I wanted to change what I was. I sensed that this endless yearning for impossible levels of connection meant that I was fundamentally lonely. I came to Japan to fix it, but nothing had changed, and I was becoming terrified that it was irreparable.

Posting pictures of yourself drunk at a night club doesn't have much relevance to how much fun your life is on any given day. Some of the worst nights of my life are immortalized in photographs where I am cheering with a drink in my hand. But watching everyone around me having an adventure while I felt doomed to a lifetime of permanent isolation certainly made Instagram a one-star iPhone app.

Of course, I came to Japan because I wanted to be alone, a secret I'd managed even to keep from myself. I'd avoided people, left my girlfriend and now I was finally alone, wanting nothing more than for someone to take a picture of me smiling with a drink in my hand having the time of my life. It was tempting to believe I had evolved: That I challenged myself every day, stormed at my fears and insecurities. Everything around me had changed and once I'd started thinking I had acclimated, I felt a comforting sense that I had changed, too.

Really, I had tricked myself into believing that I was new just because the food was. Change isn't a passive process. It's work.

Every day is a chance to practice the things you want to be, every Scary Thing is a chance to practice Scary Things. Sitting while the world changes around you, though, is still just sitting still.

I was still alone, in a room. It just happened to be in Japan.

16.
ON THE NEIGHBOR'S CHILDREN.

The neighbor's children wake up early on the weekend. They gather in the courtyard and perform a choreographed stretching exercise. Children across the country learn this routine, set to a piano piece, and the motions indicate – to me, anyway – a story about the rising sun.

On TV, I have seen postal workers perform this ritual before their morning routes, but I have only seen some real-life people do it: Some adults, and all of the neighbor's children. The children stay outside all day. They get together and play baseball or ride small plastic tricycles or, if they are older, bikes sprouting miniature wheels for balance.

One day there was a large wooden pole in the center of the courtyard. The next day a child was using it to batter the steel poles of the courtyard's fencing. The next day the plastic tricycles were strewn across the courtyard as if they were debris from a collision at adult speeds. None of the children were outside again for seven days.

On a day before I planned to travel, the door bell rang. It was very hot, and I wasn't wearing any pants. I was also in the bathroom.

I wasn't expecting anyone and wouldn't be able to communicate with whoever it was, so I stayed in the bathroom and pretended not to be home. A voice cried out in Japanese and the doorbell rang again.

The urgency and persistence of the demand was unusual for this country, and I was actually frightened by it. Someone wanted something very badly, something I would be incapable of knowing or providing. The confrontation would be awkward. It would not be said that after two years, I should probably be capable of knowing and providing whatever they needed, but I wouldn't know it, and I'd be ashamed.

I resolved to stay in the bathroom. The bell rang and the shouting resumed. I knew that they knew I was home. My behavior was now even more complicated and inexplicable. I'd done this before, in college. I was smitten with a girl and rather than act on being smitten, I waited around until she made a boyfriend and they invited themselves and a terrible dog to my house. I knew I'd be mean, so I opted to hide in the closet while they came in through the open door, asked my roommate where I was, and left.

Shortly after that I decided I needed to change my life.

Now, my front door is made of heavy metal, and it does not open or close quietly. The bell rang and then the door opened, clattering to a close but too quickly for anyone to come inside. The situation was escalating.

I knew I'd have to face the stranger or they would break into my home and take whatever they wanted, and when that feeling gave me a sense of relief, I knew I needed to get out of the bathroom and settle this, like men. I flushed.

The bell rang and the voice shouted and the door opened and the door closed, and then came the sound of the hallway door closing, the door across from the bathroom. I went into the hallway and to the front door.

Three children were screaming at me. The children had a baseball bat. Perhaps this was a robbery.

I understood the word "veranda," because in Japanese it is "berandaa." I told them to wait a minute and walked to the porch. A rubber baseball was in the gutter. It seemed too soft to play ball with. I handed it back to them.

"Gomenasai," they said. ("Sorry about that.")
"Ie deshyou," I said. ("S'alright, hey.")

Would the children have broken into my apartment to steal their ball back? In their childhoods they would have been given beans to throw at demons, usually roughly the size and stature of their parents in plastic masks. I wondered if they wished for beans today, just in case they ran into me while skittering across the kitchen to the berandaa for a deflated rubber ball.

Perhaps one of the boys was the one brave enough to lay waste to everyone's childhoods with a large wooden pole. Maybe the sense of adult destruction was crucial to his development, maybe he obliterated his own youth because it seemed so stupid to have been on tricycles and training wheels for so long, now that he has a man's game, a game with a bat and a rubber ball.

Perhaps he'd have faced me down without beans. Or maybe he'd have stayed outside. But I could tell him, if I could tell him, that the monsters I want to throw beans at the most are men-shaped adults too scared to speak if the doorbell rings while they're taking a shit.

17.
ON AWKWARDLY CONSOLING
JAPANESE SCHOOLGIRLS.

There are only so many things I know how to say in Japanese, and none of them can stop a 15-year-old Japanese girl from crying.

There's "dai joubu," and "dai joubu desu ka?" – "It's alright," and, "are you alright?" – but I'd exhausted them, along with my encouraging "ganbattes!" (persevere!) and "otsukare sama deshitas!" (you worked so hard!). She had cried for an hour by the time we'd left the convention center. A teacher was able to fill the gap for a while, but eventually I was alone with a crying Japanese teenager, tasked with walking her to the train station 20 minutes away.

It was September, almost a year after my arrival in Japan. Autumn is speech contest season, and Misaki worked for about 42 days, just one of the tens of thousands of high school kids across Japan spending their vital teenage years memorizing speeches about pets, recycling or proms.

Misaki was pretty good at English, but my advice was never simple enough. A Japanese teacher, Mrs. Kuroguchi, would translate the suggestions she agreed with. She didn't pretend to translate when she disagreed.

Over 42 days, Misaki's English improved in

fits and starts, r's emerging from "ah's" and "l's," a's slowly evolved from Japan's perpetual "san" to "can."

I've been through these contests as a witness and a judge and have felt like an executioner. There are always three-way ties for first, second and third place, and the judges usually make at least two incomprehensible decisions.

Some students sound like text-to-speech converters on Ritalin, some stand terrified and speed through their soliloquies like a skipping CD. Many sentences are forgotten and replaced by a burst of tears, the audience awkwardly shifting its gaze as the world's slowest clock ticks down to zero.

Misaki watched with hope as the text-to-speech converters and speed readers rose for the last roll call of the recitation contest winners. Then she wept for an hour and forty minutes.

Twenty of those tearful ticks of the minute hand were spent shuffling around searching for a train station. I walked too fast while Misaki kept a towel over her face and an emotional commitment to standing still.

By Fall, I could understand Japanese better than I could speak it, so I know what she told the Japanese teacher: She had practiced every day and it had come to nothing, she said. It was just like everything else she had tried: Her mid-term exams, her English tests; everything she had worked for this year. She had come so close and then fallen short. She had put in her best effort, it wasn't good enough, and she couldn't understand why.

I could relate to all of those things. It seemed to sum up my time in Japan pretty perfectly.

***

About two weeks before the contest I had crashed to the ground of my apartment, hyperventilating alone in my room with a panic attack.

I'd fallen into a heap and dialed my friend in America, where the sun hadn't risen, and I left a message punctured by gasps for breath. My heart seemed intent to pound all of my blood through my ears. I sprawled out on the tatami floor and inhaled through my nose, feeling the air run through my nose and into my lungs. I would do that, on and off, without sleep, for 48 hours.

It was more than not knowing where the sponges were in the grocery store, more than the eyes of Ms. Kuroguchi on my screen as I typed into my laptop, more than visualizing the distance from my apartment to my real friends, real friends I could not call because it was too early for them and too late for me. All of those things could make me weep, but it was a sense of tragic disappointment that kept my heart from sitting still: I had come to Japan, I had put in my best effort, and I had failed. It wasn't good enough and I couldn't understand why.

But now, Misaki was crying.

We passed a convenience store with ice cream in the window. Should I buy her an ice cream, I wondered? Ice cream is, after all, America's most elegant solution for sadness. But someone would probably call the cops. Or else Misaki would think I was weird for buying her food when she was crying, which suddenly struck me as a creepy impulse.

I had already bought her a soda that she didn't drink. I imagined sitting there with a melting ice cream cone she didn't want, either, trying to explain why I thought it was a good idea in broken Japanese. I imagined a confused look on Misaki's face before she was swept into a second wave of tears.

The real Misaki wasn't crying anymore, just staring four feet ahead of her, stopped because I had stopped. I started walking again and so did she. As soon as we passed the *konbini*, I felt awful about not buying her ice cream.

We ended up at the subway instead of the JR line because I'm an idiot. She told me we couldn't take the subway and pointed, silently, in the direction we should have walked, still staring at the ground three feet in front of her shoes.

We came to the crossway. Misaki was staring off at the sunset clouds with pink and orange bellies suspended in an azure sky.

I knew I should say something, so I did. I

gestured skyward and said either "It's beautiful, isn't it?" or "I hate it, right?" She kept her mouth closed and her eyes in the clouds.

On the train I once again asked her, "dai joubu desu ka?" and she once again replied with "dai joubu." That was all I had. The train pulled into our station and we got off. She turned to me and said, in perfect English:

"Thank you for all of your help. You have been really kind and generous."

I had kind of forgotten that she spoke English outside of the 362 words we had learned together about the healing power of pets.

"You're welcome, Misaki. Thank you for working so hard. And you did a good job."

In English I would explain that I really meant it – in English, you have to explain that you really mean things sometimes, because people are always saying things they don't mean. And sometimes they're even saying "I mean it" when they don't mean it. You can't trust anybody in English.

There was no way to tell Misaki that life is usually unfair and that hard work is not a guarantee of anything; there was no way to say that most of us spend our entire lives working really hard just to come up one point short, that sometimes everything aligns perfectly and still, somehow, gets fucked up in cruel and arbitrary ways.

There was no way to tell her it is natural and fine, that these feelings come to everyone and everyone survives: Some people even find the strength to do painfully dorky and beautiful things like practicing dance moves without music in public or reading poems out loud to the people they love or dressing cats in homemade costumes. You just take a couple deep breaths and keep moving until you die, because giving up feels worse than failing.

No 15-year-old girl wants to hear any of that. So I just said what I knew how.

"You did great. *Honto desu*," I said. ("It's true.")

She smiled for the first time in an hour and a half.

"Thank you."

18.
ON THE DEATH OF JAPAN.

The numbers say Japan is dying. There is no dispute that the Japanese get older as the children get scarcer: Ten people die for every 7 babies born. And Japan is dying in a particularly heartbreaking way: A nation that has done everything right and yet seems to be dying of loneliness.

In Nagasaki City, the population is so old that some department stores have shifted retail space for strollers and maternity dresses to display wheelchairs and canes. The streets are clean and free of graffiti, hipsters or sneaker shops. You'll find used Frank Sinatra types in the record stores instead of that vinyl Justice import.

Nagasaki sits on the west side of Kyushu, which is also aging. A recent government survey put the number of Kyushu's "Critically Depopulated Communities" (cities or towns where more than half of a population are elderly) at 2,094, up by over 400 since 2007. That's 2100 cities where the elderly are the majority. Kids leave. They go to Fukuoka, the second-youngest major city (and the second-fastest growing city) in Japan. Some go to Osaka or Kyoto. But if you start looking for the kids, you'll realize that most of them just never get born.

Most of us never get born.

***

What happens to a country that knows it is dying? People are always worried about dying. Every generation hatches some new scheme to live forever and every generation fails. The kids grow up thinking it might work until grandpa dies. Then the kids start rethinking his strategy.

Old ladies, long dead, had hoped they could be immortalized in poetry so beautiful that people would be moved for generations. Now the words are incomprehensible: Wherefore art thou Romeo?

No one takes solace in poems anymore. Write a poem and a smart girl is likely to flinch. The effort is endearing, though. Never don't write a poem for the girl. The new great hope is computers. The Library of Congress is archiving our Tweets. Fleeting whimsy forever. Wherefore art thou #Romeo?

New art changes everything, because it's a new way to live forever. Shakespeare wasn't famous for writing plays, he's famous for inventing them. Immortal artists didn't do something well. They invented something else. But if you tell an artist it's all been done, they'll get mad.

"No way. This is different. This time we're gonna live forever."

We still remember moments when a new tragedy dwarfed some earlier horror: famines, wars, holocausts. We call that history. After emerging from certain death, the human spirit erects a signpost, "We fought death and won." Beating death even once is a big deal. You may as well brag about it, and the rest of us will pay attention for a couple hundred years. We'd be happy to beat death once, too.

So we write, we sing, we paint, we record. This has been the tactic of every dead guy for the past 6,000 years. Some of those guys got lucky. Most of us don't. Japan has already stopped. Faced with the slow death of their island, the artists aren't preparing their triumphant signposts. They're leaving.

They're leaving, and so new music is being performed by computer-generated speech programs portrayed at concerts by holograms. There is a revolution underway in Japan, but it isn't concerned with falsely grabbing at immortality. It's about abandoning the body altogether.

The revolution in Japan is asexual. The academics call them "herbivorous girly men." Herbivores, as in vegetarian, which is deeply tied to Japanese spirituality. But also herbivorous for renouncing the flesh of women. These men don't play sports or slave away in competitive careers. They wander around the countryside with cameras or start funky used clothing boutiques. They're finding themselves instead of a date. In some ways, it's long overdue. Japan is dying because it's doing the right thing.

The numbers, if true, are frightening:

"About half of Japanese men aged 20 to 34 are unmarried and only 20 percent of them have girlfriends. Thirty percent have never had a girlfriend in their lives. For a country like Japan, which already has a shrinking population, this is a disaster." - The Sunday Times

Japan: A nation of boys and girls who have given up on touching each other. A nation of boys afraid to make a move.

So the boys are pioneering virtual reality porn and computer-assisted air dolls who are less emotionally complex than real women. Japanese condom manufacturers saw a 40 percent drop in sales since the Internet came to Japan.

Eventually you won't even need sex to have sex. A revolution. Surely, you say, this is unsustainable. Some biological imperative will eventually force a carnal counterstrike? Surely someone in this country wants to live forever?

Maybe. But Japan isn't facing the kind of crisis that makes it want to fight. It's not a famine, it's fatigue. A shocking 84 percent of single people in one survey said they simply weren't doing anything to find dates. A dignified culture that refuses to endure the indignities of dating. And so it is dying.

Sometimes I have visions of Japan in 2150 A.D., a country of golden shrines and red gates and robots shaped like girls the color of porcelain. Their roles are to care for the last survivor of Japan's long, dignified history of graceful decline.

Some boy born in 2050 A.D. sits in a room doing paperwork while robots run car factories, load the boats, build TVs and manage a national economy because that's what they their creators made them for.

Third-generation Japanese Americans bring their children for an Obon pilgrimage and attend to family homes maintained by robot servants. They see Shinto ceremonies performed by androids with blank faces.

The old man, the last living man born in Japan, finishes his paperwork and retires to a bath drawn by a dutiful plastic maid, eats a meal served by a dutiful plastic maid, and then settles into bed where he drifts quietly into the last dream of his life.

In the morning, a plastic servant lift him to a plastic priest for cremation, where android hands pass his bones to each other with long metallic chopsticks.

Forty days later, everything in the country stops.

19.
ON THE DISTINCT PARANOIA
OF THE SINGLE EXPATRIATE MIND.

I had a business trip and had announced to the perpetual stream of Japanese paperwork that I would leave the school at 11:50 a.m. That paper was stamped by my supervisor, the vice principal, the principal, and the business manager of the school, as is the expectation of all paperwork in the stream. However, the train schedule shifted between the time I'd filed the paper and by the time it washed back ashore on my desk. I'd have to leave 5 minutes earlier or stand 20 minutes in the rain. Assuming five minutes was an endurable adjustment, I stood up at 11:45 a.m., and asked Ms. Kuroguchi if that was OK.

She shuffled through the paperwork, saw that I had written 11:50 a.m., and the silence got tense.

"I cannot permit that," she said. "You wrote 11:50 on the business trip form."
"Yes, but the train schedule has shifted," I said.

"There's no time now to change the paper. I cannot permit it. I CANNOT PERMIT THAT."

I stood next to her silently for 5 tense minutes, then left.

Many men come to Japan to find ideal Asian girlfriends, who are rumored to be docile ego-boosters to socially awkward men. Single women in Japan do, indeed, pour our drinks, laugh at all of our jokes and tell us how strong, handsome and smart we are. And so, expat men who dated expat women were a rarity.

I was totally turned off by the idea of someone who didn't get my jokes. What are jokes for? Why be anything at all? I'm a writer and a perfectionist. I once sat at a writing desk crafting Tweets. The only way I feel valued as a human being is if someone makes out with me for being clever. Nothing else made any sense.

I wanted to kiss someone whose kiss could verify that I was still the person I thought I was, because I was starting to lose sight of it.

Being in Japan made me paranoid that I couldn't read people. So I started compulsively telling jokes, because when someone is laughing it's a clear sign that they are on your side. It also makes you look a little nuts.

***

Run too many programs on a laptop and it runs slower. There's only so much a single chip can process. In the old days you could push your luck – "overclocking the processor," a phrase that has seeped into my general understanding of anxiety.

My first months in Japan, I was overclocking the language processor, etiquette processor and the work-responsibility processor. My brain was constantly scanning the onslaught of Japanese language for the 10 percent it understood.

Unfamiliar environments breed tiny stresses – first-world problems that turn into energy sinks: Daily meetings I can't understand but am required to attend. Filling out paperwork in *kanji*, which I can't write. Going to a store and forgetting the word for the thing I need to buy. Explaining the haircut I want. Never knowing if someone said "3:15" or "3:50" but having to be on time. It is the constant presence of tiny uncertainties that make it feel like certainty about anything is impossible.

Ms. Kuroguchi never understood how I could go home four hours before her and not be fluent in Japanese. What else could I possibly be doing? I wasn't about to tell her that I was sitting in a bath tub. I tried studying Japanese, and took a weekly class, but wasn't making the progress she wanted. I was mentally drained from processing ten times as much data as she did. She'd learned how to filter out useless information from the environment, she knew what was certain and what wasn't. She was a machine designed to operate in a Japanese environment. I was not. All I knew was that routine tasks took more time and effort than

I ever expected, as if I forgot what food was every time I was in the grocery store.

I arrived in Japan with as much control over my life as a toilet-trained infant, so establishing good habits was hard. Even feeding myself was a challenge. I couldn't read menus or communicate, or communicate that I couldn't read the menus. Eventually I worked up the nerve – and enough money for an iPhone – to take photographs of the plastic food replicas in the windows.

"Kore desu," I'd say. "It's this."

Even ugly, stupid babies learn not to shit themselves, and expats in Japan are often just as capable. But doing things alone – traveling, trying a new restaurant, or exploring a new neighborhood – never crossed my mind.

I hadn't been alone for years, and now I was alone in a place where there was too much data to sort out on my own. I needed to add another processor to share the workload. That's a terrible reason for dating.

I realize now that, rather than adapting to my environment, I had adapted to my initial helplessness. That is the pernicious nature of dealing with a million tiny uncertainties in Japan: Tracking their gradual disappearance is as difficult as recognizing them. By the time you can handle them, you've learned never to be certain of anything: Hence my social paranoia. In fact, anxiety has benefits:

You can see more of the environment and process it faster. Your brain shifts to handle the accelerated rush of uncertainty by removing all its filters.

When I went home to my tiny couch and sat down with a cold glass of water, my brain was used to being juiced up. It would make up for the lack of stimulation by inventing doubts and theories about everything: It's not processing a thousand new *kanji* characters, so it would reprocess every social situation from the past week to look for stupid things I might have said. When I wasn't worried about finding my way somewhere on a Japanese map with a timetable I couldn't read, I'd shift to worrying that some girl will think I'm super needy if I ask them out to dinner.

It was difficult to trust anyone else, including myself. What had been a self-pitying loneliness became paranoia about people's private lives. I'd grow irrationally despondent when my friends kept secrets.

I've heard that expats become smarter because they can see things from multiple cultural angles. But I think there is a downside, if you haven't really mastered it. I had learned to ignore my gut feelings in a foreign culture. This adaptation had given me a perspectivelessness that made it hard to evaluate the situations I was in. I overcompensated by constantly assuming the worst.

***

Psychologists like to talk about the internal and external locus of control. An external locus leads to passive reactions to life events, because you don't feel you have any control over what happens. Fate is external, coming at you from outside.

The internal locus is the active faith in effort. You are the actor that makes things happen. Fate is the interaction between you and your environment. An external locus is "that test was too hard, so I failed," an internal locus is, "I didn't study enough, so I failed." Typically, the internal locus of control makes people happier, stressed-out overachievers. The external locus, however, sees failure as fate: You're lucky or unlucky, but we're not in charge of changing it, excepting major acts of stupidity.

We all know people whose only success is successive failure, for whom effort doesn't seem to matter. These unlucky externally focused types typically find themselves clinically depressed. After all, if it comes down to ability and luck rather than perseverance and skill, why bother applying yourself to anything at all?

We inwardly drawn neurotics are too busy gazing at our navels to notice details in the outside world. This leads to "unlucky" accidents. Imagine some sad-sack Joe shuffling his foot straight into a curb while thinking about some girl, or ramming into a car because he was daydreaming through a stop sign. Then consider the lucky people, who are always meeting interesting friends or finding amazing career opportunities. Are they "lucky?" Has some divine fox bestowed them with a brighter fate?

It's probably got nothing to do with foxes. The lucky ones are just more open to catching flirtations, suggestions and conversational doorways that lead to "lucky accidents," or, for the superstitiously disinclined, "opportunities."

If you can't communicate, you can't get things going. You can't read signs or understand your environment without a lot of extra internal processing. More fluent expats may not be unlucky on account of language, but may not see more subtle social cues: The way someone stands, or looks at you, the way you carry yourself in terms of appearing receptive to ideas, secrets and opportunities.

***

At the Fushimi Inari shrine in Kyoto, hundreds of bright red gates are crammed together, winding up the path on the side of a mountain. The gates, at first, are overwhelming and beautiful, but after a half an hour of walking they become routine. I started paying more attention to my feet, losing sight of everything around me. Even the spectacular becomes nondescript through constant exposure. Then something happens – a particular curve of the road or streak of sunlight on the paving stones. I'd wake up to where I was again, remember to pay attention and feel awed by the world. And then, inevitably, I'd stop paying attention. This is kind of the attention cycle for everything.

Here in Japan, it felt that I was always coming around corners, seeing everything the right way, learning to trust myself, and then forgetting, again.

20.
ON LOSING YOUR UMBRELLA IN JAPAN.

When the weather changes, so does your life.

In my university days, an exasperated Japanese teacher came in to greet my dripping-wet class. He asked why we were wet. "Oh that's right. Because Americans never use a fucking umbrella."

It's true. Americans don't use a fucking umbrella, because we can wear rain coats and walk to a car. It's rainy season in Japan, and because I've swapped cars for legs and trains, I've found that rain coats become miserable bags of hot sweat. An umbrella is more comfortable than a jacket. Since I've come to rely on umbrellas, I've been thinking about my connections to nature and people and fate.

If you're forced to endure nature, as I've come to be in Japan, the weather changes your life. It's not distinctly Japanese, but Shinto has elevated Japan's sense of submission to nature – if it rains, it rains. Get wet and get over it. The umbrella is a tiny concession to comfort in the face of fate, and relying on umbrellas sets off a whole chain of tiny dramas about desire and presence and connections and being rained on.

Here are five relationships I've had. With umbrellas.

1. You Were Born Without an Umbrella.

Umbrellas are never really stolen. They're paid for with a tiny story I get to tell. I'll go to a bar and say, "My umbrella got stolen." I might get a free drink out of it. The stolen-umbrella ritual of expat bonding helps me see who my friends are. "That sucks," they'll say. I don't talk about it too much, though. As with every expat conversation, it gets awkward if either of us carries on.

Umbrellas in Japan come and go. I start most days without one, find one along the way, and inevitably come home empty handed. Unlike everything else, though, I never feel entitled to an umbrella.

2. A Voyage of Self-Discovery.

I left an umbrella at the konbini and went back for it once. The women had taken the umbrella rack away. I asked if they saw my umbrella. The conversation was exclusively in Japanese, but went like this:

"Yes," she said, and stared at me.
"Can I have my umbrella?" I asked.
"Yes," she said. "Help yourself." She stared at me.
"My umbrella. I forgot it here. Did you see MY umbrella?"
"Yes," she said, smiling. "Your umbrella. We have it."

"Can I have it?"
"Yes. Help yourself!"
"OK. Sorry about this."

I lost an umbrella, but gained a realization: I don't speak Japanese very well.

3. Surviving Desire.

Sometimes I make a rational decision to leave an umbrella behind. I've abandoned an umbrella after a couple of drinks for a night of unburdened dancing. It's not an easy decision. It's like breaking up with the umbrella. It's not you, it's me. You were great, but the sky cleared up. What more can we do together?

You can have a perfect umbrella drama: You forget it, then return after the rain-soaked realization that you need it. When you come back, you found someone else had taken it home.

It's never really your umbrella, not until you lose it.

4. The One-Night Umbrella Stand.

I stole an umbrella once. It's a dirty feeling. I saw an umbrella on a wet night and I was a little drunk and I knew I wanted it more than the other guy did. I stared at the umbrella and convinced myself that taking it wasn't so bad because I'd appreciate it more. The umbrella leaned against the wall, handle cocked sideways, and winked. I got home dry but the umbrella didn't stick around for long.

It ended up disappearing in the arms of a business man outside of a konbini. If you need an umbrella, it doesn't mean the umbrella needs you.

5. Ombrelle de Jouissance.

If it's windy I use an umbrella, even when I know that it's going to break. I never care when this happens. I am heartless. No one ever thinks, "I like this umbrella. I'll protect it from this storm." I take it out and hold it sideways to stop horizontal rain. When it breaks, I toss it aside and brave the wind alone, then wish I had an umbrella the next time it rains.

To needlessly paraphrase Lacan, it's our own ego that we love in an umbrella. An umbrella makes our imaginary world seem real, at least until it breaks. In other words, you might imagine that an umbrella can stop a typhoon, but it won't.

Unless you get a really sturdy one at a upscale department store for like 6,000 yen. But no one ever buys that umbrella, do they? I'd hate to actually have my fantasy umbrella, because I'd constantly be panicking about losing it.

***

Though I don't always have an umbrella, as a foreigner it's my privilege to get stuck in the rain without being embarrassed. I get stared at, and that exasperated Japanese teacher's voice echoes through my head.

The Japanese see the weather like I see the creepy guys sweating all over each other at a bar – large, inescapable and ambivalent to anyone else's comfort. But mostly, inevitable.

Something feels more fateful, almost magical, about having the course of my day dictated by the sky. Things feel like destiny, like the Gods have intervened. I give myself the comfort of an umbrella, I hand my life to clouds. Whatever it gives me, I can't complain.

21.
ON NOT BEING
A TOTAL CREEP IN JAPAN.

The creepiness of men in Japan (homegrown and imported) has become something of a standing joke. The male expats are creepy, and it's a joke. Japanese men leer on the subway, and it's a joke. Dance floors in Japan are jokes, because women will inevitably end up grinded on or groped by someone too sketchy to "read the air."

The whole thing is a big joke, really, until it isn't. Then, people stop laughing about it, because that would mean talking about it, and nobody wants to do that. You'd upset the *wa*.

Many female expats in Japan will tell you the decks are stacked. For one, expat communities are small, and more men tend to come to Japan – especially if you factor in American military. The rest are young, recent college grads who arrive in Japan and are instantly able to find interested Japanese women.

This is a common stereotype, so I'll be careful here: I'm not saying "all Japanese women are interested in foreign men." It's untrue, and for many Japanese women, foreigners can carry a stigma. It's a small percentage of Japanese women that see foreign men as desirable, but with a smaller percentage of foreign men, it's enough.

These men do not have to be attractive. If you've ever had that borderline-racist thought that "all X look alike," that is the ally of the dorky white expat. We all look alike. If you like white guys, it's not really gonna matter. Western features are all the same.

So, even socially awkward, moderately attractive men find a steady flow of interested partners, in a complete reversal of the culture they're from. And these are aggressive women, whereas expat women tend to be comparatively aloof and selective. Traditional Western courtship begins to just take too much time.

Pick-up artists are everywhere. Braggarts are everywhere. Absolutely incomprehensible dating strategies are everywhere and work. I once watched three guys in matching goatees, top hats and cigars doing magic tricks at a club. They scored the phone number of practically every Japanese woman there, because no one could tell an exotic and interesting foreigner from a creepy clown.

Japanese men are not, as assumed, timid or afraid, or uninterested in Western women. The culture of Japan assumes women will strike up a conversation first. Though they usually don't, so there are no babies. The girl's supposed to be pouring his drinks and chatting him up. Even when the rare, Western-minded guy does approach a Western girl, the courtship can be notoriously awkward. Courtship anywhere is notoriously awkward. Dating rules are defined by culture and then refined by people – "deal breakers" vary from person to person, not city to city. I can't date a girl who says "FML" in any serious capacity, but I doubt that's true for the entire male population of New England.

Luckily, men and women usually have some overlap in the cultural norms of dating: Chivalry, in the west. Men buy dinner or whatever, flirtation commences, you lend her your cardigan and affix a carnation before asking her to prom.

Japan has no tradition of chivalry. People don't even hold the door open for each other. Japanese "dating culture" doesn't exist, because Japanese romantic rules during the West's age of chivalry were based on Samurai taking tribute from villagers, rather than wooing spoiled aristocrats with lutes.

Take a bunch of damaged or lonely people, add alcohol, stir. At its worst, the expat community is a train wreck of loneliness, alcohol, dark rooms and late-night hookups. Add aggressive men, the early end of train service, and the emotional neediness (and corresponding repulsion to that neediness) by both genders, and you have drama at best and trauma at worst.

Which takes us to an awkward and uncomfortable word. In rape cases across America, conservative statistics paint the picture clearly: 74% of rapes are committed by people the victims knew; 47% of rapes involve both parties drinking. 20% of rapes involved only the perpetrator drinking. 86% of rapes occur in the victim's home.

Staying at a friend's apartment because the trains have stopped and you're both drunk should be something a normal person could expect to do safely, but the stats say otherwise.

Coupled with the weird emotional minefield of expat anxiety and non-communicative, sexually aggressive Japanese women with inexperienced male dorks who "learn" to be aggressive in return, you don't have to be paranoid to see that this situation is prone to coercion, harassment and disaster. You'll be called paranoid anyway.

Maybe your definition of rape isn't the same as mine, but I'm not interested in that discussion. Rapists never consider what they've done to be rape. Verbal coercion, drinking with the intent of "pulling out a yes," emotional manipulation, etc, all qualify. I think we can all agree, though, that men in Japan don't have to be creeps.

So how about we just agree that if someone's passed out, they shouldn't wake up to someone trying to have sex with them, a situation a female friend of mine once woke up to. Not from some socially awkward Japanese guy with a culturally different idea of courtship (which would still be reprehensible), but by a college-educated American man in his late 20s. If someone needs a place to sleep, they should not endure 40 minutes of sexual harassment before being left alone to sleep. If you're rolling around in your own bed with a girl and she says it's time to go to sleep, shut up and go to sleep.

A study of rape-prone fraternities conducted at UPenn suggests the following formula: "The level of the perceived male peer support system for exploiting women through alcohol, plus the amount of alcohol actually consumed by men when they drink, are the primary predictors of whether they will report themselves as sexual victimizers of women."

In other words, if your friends agree that getting a girl drunk is an acceptable form of seduction, and your friends paradoxically believe that you are not responsible for the things you do while drinking, then you are more likely to get women drunk and coerce them into saying yes. Factor in other male-dominated social noise: Rape jokes, boasting, one-upmanship, etc., and you further escalate the social context for rape.

Expat men already become extreme versions of themselves, encouraged to simplify and exaggerate one's differences from other expats and from the host culture at large. This leads to extreme drinking, for one, and if we follow the formula of the study, that alone increases the risk that they'll abuse or coerce women. But the culture that grows up around male expat hives is another factor: If men are allowed to indulge in trivializing behaviors, like making rape jokes, quantifying sexual exploits, or bragging about the extremes you went to for the sake of getting laid, then that culture is going to amplify itself into a crescendo of shitty guys and shittier actions.

Men have a pretty simple task: Don't rape anybody.

If you're a guy who cares about women, you are obligated to call people out. Be a killjoy when the predatory creeps come creeping. Get in the way of unwanted groping. Make a scene when someone makes a rape joke, even if you're the only one. Especially if you're the only one. And don't, ever, buy into the new definition of consensual when it's served up by a locked-down expat culture feeding itself delusional talk about what "yes" means. It damages women, and it damages you.

22.
ON MINDFULNESS.

Japan probably has more temples, shrines and gardens per capita than garbage cans or benches.

You would think a country so heavily influenced by Buddhism would make it easy for a foreigner to stay open to the present. But life in Japan is just as distracting as everywhere else, and the reason is simple: Culture isn't distracting me. I'm distracting me.

Every morning I pass through a walking path surrounded by towering bamboo. The path gets darker and the temperature cooler and the air is filled with the sound of insects and cat-sized ravens. At the end of that path is a simple shrine.

I usually bow at the shrine before descending the heavy stone stairs to the railway crossing and into my office. Bowing bookends the start and finish of my day and briefly reminds me to stay centered in the present: Stop, look at the shrine, give up my internal yammering for however long it takes to bow. By the time I make it to the bottom of the stairs, I'm already tangled up with distractions. So much for Zen through osmosis.

It's not like I'm doing any real work. When I

bow, I'm just reminding myself that I need to get better at staying focused. You can't come to Japan, bow to a few shrines and expect it to change your life. I mean, hell, it's a Shinto shrine. I'm not even bowing to the right fox.

I've got no permanent ties to this country. I'm always aware that I'm leaving. I'm not letting roots grow, so my head tends to drift over the Pacific with alarming frequency. I'm usually thinking about Honey Nut Cheerios, cheap movies, career prospects or finally talking to girls in English. The natural order of the universe is entropy, so we're constantly being pulled away from the center of our thoughts just as the entire universe is being stretched to pieces. Our concentration is always unraveling and we're forever getting tangled in the threads. But wherever you go, there you are. Distraction-sickness happens everywhere. This is precisely the problem that Zen can help – by cultivating mindfulness.

As a child of various religious backgrounds – having attended services as a Protestant, Jehovah's Witness, "Charismatic Evangelical" (read: Speaking in Tongues), and more, I gravitated rather quickly to Buddhism in my early teens, thanks to some Shambhala Press books on the "religion" bookshelf, and had started meditating by the time I was 13.

I could list the benefits I've reaped from that period of meditation. But perhaps more important is that at the age of 15, a switch flipped and suddenly music, art, money, girls and looking cool in front of them became more of a priority than listening to my nose while searching into the darkness of my eyelids.

Meditation has been calling back to guide me out of everyday tension. I've been trying to find that mindfulness again. I'm reminded by my brief ritualistic stops at the shrine en route to work, and I've been surprised by the odd tradition in my high school of having a period of meditation before class.

So I eased back into a simple half hour of sitting and watching my body breathe, or a focused walk. I don't try to breath deeply, or regulate my breathing, or think about how I should be breathing. I just watch myself breathe, or walk, and practice being there when I'm doing it.

When my mind wanders, that's great – that's really the point of the entire practice. To rein that wandering attention back to the movement of your legs, or thinking about the air flowing through the bridge of your nose.

It's like babysitting a toddler. The kid will sit still for a while, but then run off. You can't scold her because she'll put up a struggle. But you need her to sit still, so you pick her up and gently and calmly put her back in the spot where she needs to be sitting.

The baby is my brain, and it needs to be sitting at the tip of my nose, and it needs to be listening to my breath as it moves through my nostrils. Otherwise, I am a distracted parent to myself.

Meditation is a nice practice session for daily life in the field, where I want to be present but keep drifting off. There are a lot of great opportunities to practice this in Japan, especially as I am often invited to take part in meetings I don't understand.

It will go like this:

You want to listen to your co-workers but you keep thinking about getting home and e-mailing home, or where your best friends are, and if you have time for Skyping your parents this weekend, and you wish you worked in an office where people understood your ideas and you didn't always have to simplify them into such small portions that all of your ambition to say anything at all gets lost, and you wonder if your choices are the right ones, even if you are choosing to interact with people in the right way, when there are so many ways to do things, so many paths you could have taken and can take, and sometimes it feels like you took the wrong one – and if you took the wrong path, are you stuck here, and can you get over it by going home, and maybe you will go home for holiday, or maybe you won't go home at all, wait a minute am I supposed to stand and bow yet?

Your eyes glazed over. You weren't here. You had to keep reeling yourself back into focus.

The Buddhists say that train will always take you to desire, longing and depression. That's probably true, but it also makes frequent stops at dinner plans, ice cream cravings and what-if-scenarios about being a Japanese Prime Minister. With my brain running full throttle to process more information – and to imagine ways to fill the wide holes in my knowledge of this place – the mind also tends to run into a lot of self-doubt, criticism, pessimism, and bitterness.

Meditation is the training session for re-centering attention when the train skids off the rails and crashes into stories that isolate us from the world. For me, it's seeing people and not listening to them because I've been inside of my head for a year, worrying that they notice I am not listening to them. The train gets so loud I can't hear anyone else.

I never needed a permanent megaton of all-encompassing awareness. I just wanted to catch myself when I started to drift. I wanted to remember how to be here instead of there. I wanted to control my attention span instead of having my attention span control me. I'm pretty sure my mind will wander until I die. We all will; no point in worrying. Just acknowledge it, accept it, and come back to wherever you are.

23.
ON CHERRY BLOSSOMS.

It's spring, and 4,000 kids are outside my apartment screaming about cherry blossoms. The gray and gloomy branches of last week have popped, sagging under the weight of white blossoms. I feel the weight of the cherry blossoms in my chest, hanging with hope to the trees before breezes send them streaming like confetti across the blue sky. There is no choice but to get as drunk as we can in the meantime.

From all of these trees,
salads, the soups, everything
fills up with petals.
                    - Basho

April is a complicated month in Japan. It's a time of sakura and transition, one of the few times when the internal clock of foreigners and natives tick to the same tock. April brings a new school year, and so the legions of foreign English teachers are either departing or watching staff members leave. Many expat jobs have contracts that end in April, meaning it's time for many of my friends to pack up and ship off. Teachers, however, rotate around to make sure no school keeps all the talent. Since every school should be balanced in its ratio of skilled-to-shit teachers, this means a lot of the best teachers get reassigned.

Meanwhile, new graduates are starting their first days at new companies, about to endure the team-building exercises that will mold them into proper participants in whatever corporate culture has adopted them.

Sakura blossom at this time of transition – or perhaps Japan has scheduled the time of transition to coincide with the sakura. Either way, the connection between that cherry blossom clinging to the past, and those petals all a-flutter, is a concrete one in Japanese culture: You'll find the blossoms described in haiku as old women or young children, in equal measure, because it is both within a single flower.

It blooms. It is beautiful, and heavy, but the weight of it isn't enough to save it from that wind. The weight makes the branch sloop. When I see a cherry blossom, it's always shaking, swaying on tumultuous branches, looking scared of letting go, stuck in it's attachment to an otherwise bland scrap of wood, or else it has let go and is flying about in a storm. It's born to let go of living.

Which is what Zen calls "the principle of non-attachment," the practice of letting things go. In the Zen view, the cherry blossom is a rapid cycle of birth, attachment, and surrender. We're born wanting stuff, and the tragedies of our lives are built around not getting that stuff. The blossom wants to stay on the branch. But we know it won't. When it lets go, take it as a lesson.

When Basho wrote about Haiku for the

aspiring beatniks of his day, he told them that the core of the haiku is loneliness, sabi, half of that glorious phrase wabi-sabi, which I'll half-heartedly describe as the mix of loneliness and ecstasy felt in those brief moments where you're OK with the heaviest meaning of passing time. That fleeting sense that hey, we're all gonna die someday, and it's going to be alright. Sakura is wabi-sabi's high season.

I've heard wabi-sabi described as a joke on foreigners, something Japanese people rarely discuss unless explaining Japan to outsiders. My guess is it probably doesn't come up much, just as I (or, well, a normal person) would never sit around talking in English about melancholy. It's a personal thing and talking about it defeats the purpose.

Unless you're a poet. There are festivals where sake floats down a river, and you fetch the sake, compose a poem, read the poem and take a shot. Then you put the poem on the float and send it away.

The spring rituals soothe my anxiety. They serve as markers of the times before, the tribulations that I once believed were insurmountable, and how little they seem to matter now, just a year after the last blossoms dropped to the grass. In my personal life, when faced with most major transitions, I, for one, never seem to believe that it will be better than what has come already. I make a lot of stuff up about the future – good and bad, hopeful and catastrophic – then painfully yearn for those things to materialize. I gotta let go of the branch.

Things are changing all the time. April in Japan crams all of that uncertainty into a single season, marked by the arrival and departure of sakura blossoms. The cycle is comforting. Everything changes and then the cherry blossoms scatter and you start again until they bloom and fall again. The catastrophes that I've envisioned – the root of my anxieties – have come to pass, and yet here I am, again, drinking beer in a storm of petals.

If I get anxious about how perfect life would be if things had gone some other way, it helps to remember that I've been through this cycle before. Then I draw some tea or go for a run. And in a few hours, or days, or months, I'm fine. I've done another lap on another year's anxieties, will do it again, and most likely I'll continue to survive.

The moon, the blossoms
This and that and this and that,
That's just how it goes.
- Issa

Like cherry blossoms, we're taken for a ride through the tension and the stomach drops and ecstasies and heartache and most of it is this terrifying onslaught of life followed by life followed by more brutal, shaky, beautiful life. We can look at those fuckin' trees and if you could ask them they'd tell us, life and the rest of it is just as beautiful when you're clenching your fists as when you're letting it go.

It was time to loosen my grip on the things I wanted – time to stop grasping for someone else to come along and help me.

24.
ON RUNNING IN JAPAN.

For the listener, who listens in the snow,
And, nothing himself, beholds
Nothing that is not there and the nothing
that is.
  - *Wallace Stevens, "The Snowman"*

I've been independent my entire life, and here I am in a completely dependent society, a writer – and reader – turned illiterate and passive in a land full of passive communicators. Japan loves when you are polite and vague, draped in an elegant and exhausting uncertainty.

All of this, according to American psychologists, is a recipe for anxiety. At least, for Americans. I assume the worst. When I'm given responsibility over a mystery, I brace for cataclysms instead of realistic outcomes. When I can't say what we want directly, I feel like no one can understand what I need.

I spent a lot of time in the bathtub watching the water rise as I inhaled and drop as I exhaled, sending steam into spirals as I sat sweating with a pastel-colored lamp shaped like an egg. It was meditation as relaxation – the kind of meditation you might practice at a spa.

I sat in the bath and breathed out my anxiety. Then I'd stand up, towel beads of water from my shoulders, and sleep. I'd spend the next work day bombarded with polite imprecision. I'd walk home from work and find my breath getting shorter from tension, and soak in the bath.

I was tired of it. I'd exhausted all my friendships by demanding infinitely more than any friendship could be expected to provide. Everyone, it seemed, was sick of my problems – and, finally, so was I.

In a sort of counterbalance to my deep sense of stagnation, I started running. I bought a blue and green track suit with a slogan that would only be inspirational in Japan: "I do not try, and I do not find success." I wore this track suit with the only cold-weather hat I had, which is part of a hamburger costume. I was Mayor McCheese on a fitness campaign, scaring off the stray cats picking through the rubbish by the lake.

Running is a good example of practice in the Buddhist sense, because the thing you are practicing is also the thing you are doing. I have to tell my doubts to shut up so I can do the things I want to do but don't want to do. I practice this over the course of 5-8 kilometers 1-3 times a week. Every time I put a foot in front of the other, I beg myself to stop. Then I ignore it.

Mindfulness meditation is about being present. I tried to practice with my eyes open. I'd sit comfortably, watch my anxiety float up and then remind myself that the anxiety was a story – that I was inventing my planet, then freaking out about it.

The problem with mindfulness meditation is that it's boring. Everyone tells me that I should transcend that boredom, but frankly, the boredom made me anxious. And while I'm sure I could, eventually, liberate a million souls into enlightenment with proper training, I felt like the first priority was to stop freaking out about losing control over nearly every aspect of my life.

So, I ran. And I adopted my mindfulness practice into running.

Mindful Running - which ought to be the name of a new-age fitness bestseller - is entirely about controlling the story you tell yourself while running. In standard meditation, you let anxiety come and go, focused on the breath coming in over the ridge of your nose.

With running, it's your entire body. Your legs are tired, but your brain says they are more tired than they are. You feel cold air sting your lungs, and tell yourself that you will run more when it is warmer. You feel out of breath and tell yourself you have to stop. But you keep running.

When I started running, I just sprinted. I'd assume that a proper workout meant pounding my lungs and heart into an exhausted mash for as long as I could. That's what I'd call mindless running. Mindful running is about pacing. You get better at pacing the more you practice, and you have to practice to understand pacing. Eventually you know how your legs need to move to sustain a long run, and you can push it harder or keep it slower, depending on the demands of the terrain. Your legs are your ally here. Your legs cut off your internal narrative and tell you: "Listen. Shut up. We're busy, and we need that energy to run."

I've learned to do this with my anxiety. Rather than fighting it until it bursts out into the hot water of the bath, I've started to look at my anxiety and devise a strategy for pacing my way to a somewhat more benign form of hysteria.

At the start of a run, you have all this energy. You feel like you need to sprint. One of the first things I learned as a new runner was to resist the temptation to burst.

From giving you a panic attack or low-level neurosis to making you think maybe you should stop running and go get some pastries, your brain hates everything about you and wants you to fail. What your brain wants is to be safe, comfortable, warm and well-fed. Anxiety is your brain's way of making sure you stay swathed in a down comforter eating chocolate ice cream in your apartment for the rest of your life. Loneliness is your brain's way of making sure you don't wander too far away from the people who can give you food.

Your legs, as a runner? Your legs are busy doing the stuff that your brain is telling you it can't do.

I needed to practice arguing with my anxiety. Running is just a series of arguments with the part of your brain that wants you to stop running. I look forward to running now and in some perverse ways I have started to look forward to other sources of stress for the same reason. It gives me the chance to practice. I started to see stressful places and people as opportunities to practice overcoming anxiety.

Approaching everything as a chance to practice, everyone became a perfect player. As you might choose to run a steep hill without giving into exhaustion, you might choose to have a difficult conversation without giving into resentment. Like a hill, they will be perfect even when they are terrible, because you get to practice. Hills, and people, are always playing their roles perfectly. Even when you fail, you get better.

Eventually, as you run, you stop being at war with your entire body. And if you allow yourself to practice, you will become mindful of the choices you are making with every step, in spite of every part of you giving you an excuse to stop – you can feel the difference in your clarity of thought.

Suddenly, I noticed herons reflecting on the still pond or the sun setting on lounging cats. For a series of ever-expanding moments, it's not about your breath, or the impact in the knees or the crush of sneaker cushioning on your feet. The argument goes away, and you're just there, moving through it, seeing nothing that is not there, and the nothing that is.

I shower, of course, but I haven't had a bath in months.

25.
ON CLIMBING MT FUJI.

About 300,000 people a year climb Mt. Fuji. A handful of them die. Very few of them get panic attacks from standing on porches.

I'm acrophobic: Seven feet high and I'm nervous. Higher up I get dizzy; at 30 feet my heart races and beyond that I get sparks in my eyes. My body spikes with adrenalin and I can't stand or speak coherently. If I go higher, I might black out. It's like being drunk, if you replace easy laughter with vertigo. Reasonably speaking, I had no business climbing the side of a 12,400-foot mountain.

Our plan was ambitious enough: I'd sleep until 1 p.m., catch a plane to Tokyo and travel nonstop to Mt. Fuji to hike overnight, starting at 9 p.m. and finishing at the peak by sunrise. That plan began unraveling when the milk salesman rang my doorbell at 9 a.m. and shouted "Ohayo Gozaimasu!" five times. I don't even drink milk.

My friends and I flew from Fukuoka to Tokyo and arrived 22 minutes late. Call it the Milkman's curse. We literally ran through the airport to a taxi whose driver chuckled when we told him what time our bus left. We ended up missing the tour bus from Shinjuku to Mt. Fuji by exactly 3 minutes.

We hatched a plan. We left Shinjuku for Matsuda Station by subway (2 hrs) and then took a train to Gotemba (1 hr). By this stage it was midnight and the station closed behind us, leaving us stranded with a kid breakdancing in the corner.

That's when we found our bad-ass taxi driver. He said he'd take us for the hour-long trek by highway to the base of Mt. Fuji for 27,000 Yen ($330 USD). He also took us to a conbini, where I ate an egg salad sandwich, my first meal since curry rice eleven hours earlier. The cab driver speeds and points out deer on the highway. He says he was a cop.

The fifth station marks the start of the Yoshida trail, which goes to the summit. There are only a handful of coin lockers and they're full, so I'm stuck carrying a three-day supply of books, cameras and clothes up the side of Mt. Fuji.

I also packed a headlamp, a 2-liter bottle of water, a smaller bottle of sports drink, gloves and extra layers of clothing. I wore sneakers, which everyone told me was insane, but nobody ever thinks anybody's shoes are good enough for Mt. Fuji.

We took a half hour to stretch and acclimate to the thinning oxygen. Then, at 1:45 a.m., we chugged a red bull and started climbing.

Fuji starts out as a downhill slope from the station. You wander along giant walled paths with forests of twisted tree roots. For the first part of the climb you might get cocky. If the climb is going to be like this, what's the big deal? What idiot said I needed hiking boots?

I had energy and I was pretty sure that energy was going to last forever. I hadn't seen much of the mountain but what I had seen was simple. I assumed, based on limited observations, that the entire climb was going to be easy, just long, and I had no idea why anyone else has ever warned me that it was hard.

I'd adopted the casual arrogance of a teenager. That changed after I bought a 200-yen banana from a mountain hut.

Along the trails are a number of service huts run by crazy mountain people or college interns. We came to the first one at 3:11 a.m. and I bought a banana. After that, the trail turned from a roughly 20-degree incline to something much steeper, and terror sweat began to flush out of my pores.

Here is how the fear works: In high-up spaces, I become convinced that falling is normal. My rational mind can't remember the last time I fell down, but my acrophobic mind says it happens all the time. Furthermore, the space between my body and the ledge shrinks. Ten feet away may as well be 10 inches. Rationally, I know that if I fell, I'd have to roll 5-6 times to go over the edge. My fear thought that would be easy to do on accident, because once you fall how can anyone stop themselves from rolling forever? In my fear-addled brain, falling off of the side of a mountain meant falling all the way to the base. As if the momentum from rolling would break through anything that stopped me from falling. In reality, you'd typically just fall 7-20 feet to the trail below and stop. Maybe you'd break a leg, or arm, or, if you're very unlucky, your neck.

Fear of heights is not about leg-breaking, it's about death. Climbing Fuji was my way of coping with that fear. It wasn't supposed to be easy. The inclines were supposed to be steep.

By starting in the darkness, I had some time to get acclimated. I was still terrified as the sun began to rise, but I knew better than to move my head up or down. To get any perspective would send me into a downward spiral of weak-kneed paralysis. So I stared at the rocks and braced myself for the coming daylight. At 3:45 a.m. the sun came up, as it does.

The sky turned red; the climb got steeper, the drops got brighter, my heart beat faster. I was desperate to get distance between myself and whatever stone I stood on, because every stone contained the threat of falling. I would say I ran up the first few inclines after the sun came up, but it was more like a hurried crawl, like an idiotic Spiderman. I was full of adrenalin and testosterone. I was desperate to hurry up and reach the summit so I could stop being afraid of where I was.

I was being passed by grandmothers and schoolchildren on holiday. This drama in my head was nothing to them. I remembered when I'd wait in line for the Roller Coaster at theme parks, usually to impress some girl, and break into a cold sweat while the middle school kids in front of me made fart jokes, in line for their third ride that day. I understood that being afraid of being thrown through the air at breakneck speeds for pleasure is something rational people can choose to do. I despised having that choice, "no," made on my behalf by something within me that I couldn't control.

On Fuji, I kept my eyes on the stones. That's when I figured it out: Stop observing what frightens you, and start observing your fear. Your fear will tell you to think about what you are doing, give you great incentives to stop, spell out worst-case scenarios. Tune it out. You'll never stop hearing it, but you can stop listening. You can let it prattle on in the background while you focus on which rock you will step on next.

The inclines ease for a bit and my fears went with them, but I felt the limitations of my body instead. I couldn't take two steps without fighting tired knees, thighs and ankles. Blisters, accumulated over hours of climbing without regard for your toes, finally started to burst and slow me down.

Bees started appearing. It's bewildering, because there were no flowers. Or life of any kind. There is no pollen, only Nalgene bottles. But there are bees investigating whether I am a flower, and when they see I am not a flower, they look somewhere else where flowers aren't.

We passed the white torii gate at about 9:00
a.m. into a makeshift shanty town. The
restaurant serves ramen and curry rice and
you eat it on the floor. It was my first meal in
13 hours and had to make up for about 7200
calories. I used a toilet – 200 yen up the
mountain, 300 yen at the summit – and fell
asleep for half an hour staring at a box of
used toilet paper.

I stood for a moment at the edge of a
volcanic crater and watched steam rise. Then
I turned around and started walking, my
accomplishment overwhelmed by exhaustion
and the sad awareness that the top is not the
end. It's the half-way point. It's fine that you
climbed Mt. Fuji and everything, but you still
gotta get down.

The walk down the mountain is just enough
to keep you from standing up straight. It's
covered in what my sleep-deprived mind
hallucinated as all the colors of the monster-
cereal rainbow: Frankenberry, Booberry and
Count Chocula. The landscape turns red and
dust starts kicking up as people slide. I
walked with a towel over my mouth; my pant
legs turned purple; even the items inside of
my bag became a weird rust-brown.

I cursed my shoes. The lack of grip made for
6 hours of taking one step and sliding three
feet, possibly falling backward, forward, or
off of a cliff. As the shoes slid down the
mountain with a canyon three feet to my
side, this was literally the stuff of my

nightmares: Slippery earth near steep drops. And yet, here I was, not dizzy, not blacking out, just really angry about my shoe decision.

You can descend Fuji without falling, but you have to run. The ground slides and carries you about a foot each time you take a step, but you have to work on your next step while you are sliding. The front of your shoes are digging into crushed volcanic ash in the process, and if you are wearing sneakers, the dust and rocks will get in your shoes and socks. Your feet will bleed; you will blister, your skin will burn for a day or two.

All of this pain might not matter, because if it is a clear morning and the weather is right, you will start running directly into clouds. These are not some weird clouds that hang out next to mountains. These are "the clouds," the ones you see from the ground and wish you could touch, because they would be so soft and cottony. You can reach your hand out on Fuji and touch them: A dark, dense concentration of condensation, filled with the electric mist of pre-rain air. Cotton balls of petrichor.

If you believe in God then maybe you will think you're going to run into Jesus; and if you do not believe in God, then maybe it's enough just to touch a cloud. Maybe you wanted to do that as a kid, but you shrugged it off because touching clouds is impossible, like touching the moon or capturing a unicorn or riding a dinosaur. It doesn't really matter if you think it's heaven or you think it's just a cloud. It doesn't matter if you are wearing boat shoes or hiking boots. Either way, you're totally walking in the sky.

I reached the "bottom" of Mt. Fuji with blistered feet, sore shoulders and hallucinations, after 24 hours without sleep. My relief quickly turned to stoic resolve when a map informed me I still had to complete a 3-hour circumnavigation of Mt. Fuji's base before I got home.

It's the path I walked through when I started. I was walking through the stomping grounds of my old Red Bull-fueled arrogance in a hallucinogenic daze. Finally, back at the trail head: It's unrecognizable. The shops are open, people are everywhere, there is ice cream and souvenirs. But there are no chairs.

Our bus back to Tokyo gets stuck in traffic. My dreams felt like 9-hour days in themselves. I'd wake up, see 10 minutes had passed and doze off again, building a week of dreams out of islands of sleep.

Back in Shinjuku, before I took a shower, I looked at my body: I'm covered in dirt. There's red sand in my beard. My teeth are brown with two days of curry and dust, my hair is the texture of a guinea pig – it stands straight up like a bouffant. My nose is ringed with black dirt and pimples. My beard is patchy. My arms and neck are sunburned in weird swirls because I was terrified of stopping to properly apply lotion. I have four blisters on my toes, which are black from creeping volcanic dust; I have black bags under my eyes from exhaustion, and four bruises over my body.

Climbing Mt. Fuji is like falling from an airplane on foot. Fuji is immortal and it is inexhaustible. It was without a doubt the most difficult thing I have ever done, and while it was rewarding, there is a saying about Mt. Fuji that is famous for everyone who walks it: "Only a fool doesn't hike Mt. Fuji. Only a fool does it twice."

26.
ON LONELINESS.

Most people do not move to a foreign country where they don't speak a word of the language, but then most people are not resigned to loneliness. Lonely people are social telecommuters: It doesn't matter where we are, because we'll feel lonely anyway. May as well get some decent green tea while we're at it.

Not everyone who moves to Japan is lonely when they arrive, but most are by the time they leave. One can't reasonably complain about it, of course: We do it to ourselves. But we can try to understand how loneliness works – and we have plenty of opportunity to study that question in Japan.

Some people are born lonely. As a lonely person, articulating this difference can be difficult. Lonely people seem depressed to non-lonely people, and sometimes we are. We are perfectionists, striving for an impossible level of connection and disregarding anything that falls short. We are wary of new people, who require a lot of energy. It's tiring for lonely people to extend themselves into non-loneliness, too hard to finesse anything less than a perfect click of personalities.

Lonely people, I've found, are more likely to make music or read poems or get lost in fiction. Art pitches itself to a niche audience of lonely people. We can't articulate to a specific person, so we articulate to the world at large. No one tells us what we want to hear, so we ask dead poets. We cultivate interior landscapes and wonder why we are, so frequently, trapped in our own weeds.

The layman's idea of loneliness is tied to rejection: You're undesirable. But that's secondary. Instead, we feel wasted. We've explored an inner wilderness but nobody cares to see the map. We have erected libraries in there, with books and quotes and short films of symbolic significance. All this stuff that goes into the construction of our self, the symbols that seeped in and took root. It inspires empathy, because we know that every person has the same thing, but it also inspires frustration, because we don't know how to explore it with anyone else.

I imagined I'd find a manageable kind of loneliness in Japan. My isolation was largely self-imposed. I'd make the map and it would be OK, I'd carve out some new landscapes. I'd do it deliberately, so rejection would have nothing to do with it. But as one grows accustomed to life abroad, this sense of self-imposed ostracism loses its protective charm. One meets people who seem open to trading cartography advice, but it never happens, or it happens superficially. Cartography conversations seem ever important and ever unsatisfying.

Art, like a mountain, was once the great

common reference of internal mapmaking. You meet someone and they show you this album or movie or book or song or poem or whatever, and then the two of you agree that yes, you both have seen it, and without realizing it, you can look at the trails that got you there. It's exciting but soon wears out. Art is ever so localized.

"Yeah, they're pretty good."

Art, at least when giving directions to our inner life, is a distressingly poor landmark.

Loneliness, according to its earliest researchers, was defined as the unfulfilled desire for intimacy. So, we are drawn to the kind of social events that might loosen the barriers: get drunk, hook up, stop being alone by being in someone's arms, even if they're kind of a terrible person.

***

Science knows some things about loneliness.

Science knows that, in the absence of social stimulation, we seek mental stimulation anywhere we can, whenever we can. Psychologists agree that lonely people smoke, overeat, drink too much and engage in "indiscriminate sex" more often than those with satisfying social connections.

Science knows that loneliness, borne of stress, inspires stress. Loneliness increases already high levels of stress hormones. It makes us more susceptible to disease. Lonely people feel daily stress more deeply, and unexpected problems experienced in isolation can be surprisingly debilitating. Welcome to Japan.

Science knows that loneliness is self-fulfilling. If we feel lonely at work, which seems to be inevitable, we carry it home. I carried it into the bathtub, until I read enough to stimulate the social connection part of my brain.

Science knows that we crave intimacy more just as we imagine that no one is interested in what we have to say. Indeed, in an act of biological irony, the most difficult time to trust people is when we need to trust people the most. Vulnerability breeds defensiveness; rejection stings more. But also, it turns out, lonely people are worse at reading faces. We pick up on negative social cues more than positive ones. I found Japan's vague sense of communication (and facial expressions) a constant assurance that I was a nuisance and a burden to everybody who had to talk to me.

***

In 1978, researchers at UCLA devised a simple questionnaire to measure loneliness. Twenty statements, rated on a scale of intensity. The statements read almost like a check list for living in Japan.

On a scale of 1-4, evaluate: I have nobody to talk to. I lack companionship. I feel that nobody understands me. I find myself wanting people to call or write. My ideas are not shared by anyone around me. I feel left out. I am unable to communicate with those around me. My social relationships are superficial. No one knows me well. It is difficult to make friends. I feel excluded. People are around me, but rarely with me.

These statements are objectively true. OK, OK, I know: Boo-hoo.

But the Japanese expat life is an inherently lonely one, and once you start to see it in people, you start to get sad. Native-language social interactions are extremely rare compared to home. When I interacted with other people in Japan – particularly, but not exclusively, other expats – they were lonely too. We'd get together, feel needy and inspire a mutual, secret panic.

I wanted intimacy, but was terrified of scaring people away. I started over-thinking social strategies. I feigned aloofness, then pushed boundaries of intimacy, then panicked when people reciprocated. I'd pull away, my feigned aloofness becoming real, and then panic, then wonder whether I was crazy or someone else was. We both were.

Lonely people, according to research, crave intimacy but actually loathe self-disclosure. We want to be accepted, which makes the stakes of rejection all the more terrifying. We get anxious and defensive, isolate ourselves from people we want to talk to.

We won't talk. We need to talk, in fact, we want to cram a week's worth of social warmth into a single blaze of one-sided conversation. And we inevitably will. After a few pints, I would tear down social barriers to intimacy at an unsettling pace. It's easy to force it, to demand it out of the people closest to me, even if it's just not there. The minute I started talking, I started to feel like I was terrifying everybody.

For a while I went to work every day assuming I was disliked by my co-workers. I didn't trust that they were being honest with their kindness, I assumed they were being nice. Nice wouldn't have cut it anyway. I craved intimacy, and my limited Japanese made it impossible.

People told me, "If you learn Japanese, you can make more friends," but you can only talk about food for so long before you start getting hungry for something else. Studying wouldn't have helped. I wouldn't be having the conversations I wanted to be having, because I wanted to have impossible conversations.

There is no conversation that would have fixed it, and there is no connection that could be reached over a pint or a night in bed with anybody. There is nothing anyone can say to make lonely people feel like other people are sharing themselves, because there is nothing we will hear through our own pulsing desire to disclose something ourselves. I would sense, if you told me a secret, that you immediately regretted telling me, because that's how I'd feel.

Acts of social sharing that should be deeply fulfilling leave lonely people feeling less satisfied than the non-lonelies.

***

There's that old Zen story about a student who seeks enlightenment from a monk. The student sits down with a hot cup of tea and talks, at length, about the things he has studied, the many masters he has met, the experiences he has had, the threats he has survived. He talks and talks, until his tea turns cold. "Why, then, can I not find enlightenment?"

The Zen master nods, and begins to pour fresh tea into his cup. The monk keeps pouring as hot green tea rises over the brim, into the saucer, to the table and down onto the floor.

"The cup is you," says the monk.

We have this metaphor that loneliness is emptiness. That we are an empty bottle that needs to be filled. But my loneliness was never the result of being empty. I had way too much stale tea in my cup: Old fears, old insecurities, imaginary threats. I assumed I needed to pour my heart out to someone, and maybe I did, but I couldn't trust anyone to listen.

Loneliness was a paradox because it meant keeping an inner life that was so full that it was unwieldy and esoteric. I'd have a hard time connecting to other people because of all the clutter. I wanted them to speak not just English but also the language of the books I'd read, the ideas I considered fundamental. The reason people were exhausting is because I had no room to hold their tea. And when people spoke to me – if they were really looking – they would see my eyes glaze over as every word they said spilled immediately out of my cup and onto the table.

So rather than seeing people as vessels to pour myself into, I started looking at all the cold tea I needed to swallow or spit out. I was alone because I was keeping people away.

When people say "you have to let people in," it has that patronizing feel of country song wisdom, like we're all tragic teenagers who, if only we "let people love us," would be transformed into people who gazed lovingly at hand-made scrapbooks.

I really was full of myself, the end result of living immersed in a world I'd made in isolation. I wanted to talk for hours to someone else just to prove that I was here, just to have some witness to my existence. To verify that I was real, by relating to them, so I could be remembered and understood.

We lonely people have spent our lives out in the world gathering sticks and roots, berries and books and cinema and snippets of poems and boys or girls we crushed on and the memories of how we nursed away that rejection. We've collected moments of symbolism, snapshots in our head of pleasant and meaningful memories, and added them to a pestle, ground them up into a powder, and stirred them into hot water with a bit of milk.

We've tried to offer that cup of tea to everyone we meet. It's fresh and hot at first, when we're young and able to offer it up to anyone who asks.

We get older and fewer people ask. We still want to spill that cold tea into someone else's cup – not for the joy of sharing, but so that they can carry it with them, so they can remember that we were capable of brewing such fine tea – and we hope that they will taste the complex richness that we know must be there.

But when we're lonely, we refuse to let go of our attachment to ourselves. We lose the drive of our curiosity. I wanted share myself so badly that I left no room to be shared with, then panicked that nobody ever told me anything.

All this bitter tea – cold and stale, undrinkable, unwanted but carried around because we grew the leaves and brewed them on our own. Drink it or pour it down a drain, but somehow, we've got to empty that cup before we can expect anyone else to serve us another, before we can begin collecting another bunch of ideas and berries and brew them into something that we actually want to drink.

When that cup is quite warm, we can offer it,

freely, to someone else, and take in some of theirs.

27.
THE NEUROTIC'S
TRAVEL GUIDE TO KYOTO.

SHIJO DORI.

Some might say that Kyoto is not about romance. There are temples and shrines everywhere, some of the oldest in the country, and so Kyoto could be considered the spiritual heart of Japan. But as the sun sets on the Kamo river, its beds are flanked with a thin black line of hand-holding couples. At dusk you can step into any alley and find a narrow maze of lanterns and stone paths leading to restaurants that bleed red wine through sliding paper doorways.

As a solo traveler it's hard not to cringe as I sit alone at a shop with dim lighting, staring out the window at a canal, expensive pizza en route and a glass of wine to get me started. Out comes the iPod and the prompt download of the OK Cupid application.

My time spent traveling alone in Thailand taught me the lesson of gratitude at the expense of an anxious longing for what I'd imagined I "ought to have." Kyoto is a direct challenger to that progress.

After one night in the black and red dimly lit neighborhoods of Gion, and I understood why men pay women in white makeup to pour drinks and laugh at their jokes.

"Love in action is a harsh and dreadful thing compared with love in dreams. Love in dreams is greedy for immediate action, rapidly performed and in the sight of all. Men will even give their lives if only the ordeal does not last long but is soon over, with all looking on and applauding as though on the stage. But active love is labor and fortitude, and for some people too, perhaps, a complete science." – The Brothers Karamazov

If Dostoevsky were an urban planning expert, he might have described my Kyoto as the city of love-in-dreams. Everywhere there's some temptation to do something bold in the name of love. The air is crisp and small canals reflect paper lanterns along the streets. If Kyoto were swapped with Paris most poets wouldn't notice.

But Kyoto is love in dreams, a city of projections. With imagination, the city could be anything. You don't even know this city, man. How can you say you love it?

GION.

There's an apparition moving at me. There's something ethereal about her shoulders. They don't shift when she walks. Somewhere below her kimono there might be a skateboard, but I know it's wooden sandals, *geta*, and she's moving through the crowd with poise and carefully maintained speed. I lift my camera to get a photo but the damn lens can't focus, and suddenly she's floating left instead of right; zigging where she should have zagged.

If you see geisha, or *maiko*, you'll start to crack my theory of Kyoto. The city, like the women who famously live there, promise an impossible ideal. It's like the worst kinds of crushes I've had on waitresses and baristas, the ones where I know I'm making it all up, the ones where I know I'm projecting a ghost on a girl and not seeing the girl in front of me.

Which seems to be the entire allure of geisha. If you have indulged in that capacity for love-in-dreams, maybe you understand the allure of paying a woman to laugh at your jokes and play the harp. Some men can understand prostitution – you pay for a service in which the rumpled bed sheets prove that something physically has transpired. But paying for the illusion of love? Intangible, ethereal, wispy love? No wonder my lens can't find her, she's cultivated to be a walking Gaussian blur.

For the romantics, paying for sex doesn't make any sense. Paying for a human screen to project a dream on for a lifetime, though? Paying someone for the thrill of impossibly longing for them? To maintain a love in dreams that will never become that dreaded love in action?

That's worth some money.

SANJUSANGENDO.

"It is much, and well that your mind is full of such dreams and not others. Some time, unawares, you may do a good deed in reality." – The Brothers Karamazov.

In the southeastern bit of Kyoto, near Kiyomizudera, there's a long wooden hallway with 1001 life-sized Buddhas painted gold. They line the back walls in rows, five high, standing on rafters like basketball parents watching a high school tourney. Along this hallway are five statues of various Buddhist icons, famous monks or spirits, slightly larger than life-size in the case of the men, but 100 percent accurate sizes for the supernatural beings.

It was 10 a.m. on an arbitrary week in autumn and no one was in the temple. The warrior spirit, Fyudo Myu, was alive and well in darkened bronze. We've been old friends since I met him in the Buddhist temple at the Museum of Fine Arts in Boston. He's that badass friend of yours who learned early on that he'd have to be responsible with his strength.

In real life he'd be a noble bouncer.

Fyudo Myu has a noose to drag me through my delusions. It's ironic, then, that I swore I saw him breathing. The statues' eyes are crystals, like staring into human eyes. They seem to move. I have to imagine that it's this human habit of finding human faces – the man in the moon, Jesus in the pita bread – that tricked me into seeing that slight heaving of his chest. In Kyoto, geisha don't breathe, but the statues do.

I don't know if you've ever been recruited into an organization that plans vaguely cult-like weekend seminars for self-actualization, but if you have, you might be familiar with the experience of staring into the eyes of 20 complete strangers for ten minutes each.

It is the purest form I've experienced for catching on to the heaps of bullshit that I project on people: "Are they angry? Are they sad? Is this woman in love with me? I feel like she's in love with me. Oh shit, who's this guy?"

The same thing happened when I stared at the supernatural beings.

"He looks sympathetic."
"He looks scary."
"He has nine eyes and it's freaking me out."

The centerpiece of the temple is a single sitting Buddha as tall and wide as ten of the soccer-mom Buddhas standing on the rafters. While this is a historical tourist attraction, it is still a temple, and so it is still a place where you can light incense and meditate. A sign suggests, "Let's pray for our loved ones."

Which I am always skeptical of doing, despite my Buddhist leanings, but thanks to reading *Eat Pray Love* I figured I could indulge in meditating at a tourist attraction temple and then writing about it.

***

The challenge of my anxiety – my frayed social connections, the isolation and loneliness of life as an expat in Japan – has been to find its root and weed it out. By withdrawing from the somewhat insular world of the English-speaking expat community where I live for a handful of days in Thailand, I'd learned a thing or two about being alone, namely, that it is not the terrifying simulation of death I'd assumed it to be. Or, more accurately, it is precisely a simulation of death, but death is a lot more fun if you do it right.

In Thailand, I met people on the road in a perfect kind of friendship, because we were together long enough to enjoy the company but never long enough to develop expectations. I often struggle with gratitude towards people. I remember as a child, telling my father that I remembered what I saw before I was born. It was the absence of anything at all, I said, like closing my eyes except there wasn't even darkness.

I was making all of that up, but I remember that conversation, and it strikes me now that I never took that story – as firmly as I believed in it – and extrapolated out to a realization that I was remarkably lucky to not be nothing any more. The idea that I got to be *something* is pretty awesome, the idea my life has happened in contrast to nothing happening is something to appreciate.

Rather than gratitude, though, I've come to expect a lot out of people before they go back to nothing. I'd meet people over a few days in Thailand and then they'd go. A lot of them were alright. A lot of them were problematic. Most of them were gone by my next meal. It's a brilliant exercise in suspending expectations and just letting people connect with the one thing you can both share: Your own temporariness.

I expect a lot from people I know in Japan. I kind of have to. But after a few days of ephemeral friendships I just felt happy that the people I know here in my life for years, and not days, and not hours.

In Japan, I am floating adrift with loose ties, trying to look outside for a rock to be tethered to. Finding none, I panic. I have lacked a grounding sense of grace. When I have needed grace, I've demanded it from other people and drifted. Of course I'd be anxious.

In Kyoto, surrounded by 1000 Bodhisattvas, I kept eye contact with the Buddha and imagined the face of everyone I knew, for a cycle of two breaths, and allowed myself to feel grateful for their presence in my lives. Even the douche bags and the shits, the ones just as crazy and desperate and sad as I am.

I stared into the crystal eyes of a towering Buddha, watched it breathe, breathed with him, cultivated love and serenity, broadcast my goodwill outward, and my entire world transformed into the album art for a 60's psychedelic rock compilation.

YASAKA SHRINE.

There is no ignorance, and no end to ignorance. There is no old age and death, and no end to old age and death. There is no suffering, no cause of suffering, no end to suffering, no path to follow. There is no attainment of wisdom, and no wisdom to attain.

The Heart Sutra is 16 sentences (in English) and is said to be the fundamental sutra of Mahayana Buddhism, the devotional branch. It's one of the few sutras Buddha doesn't get the credit for. It was written before the Buddha was even born, because Buddhism existed under different names before Buddha summed it all up for us.

The sutra forms a core part of Buddhist practices from Tibet to Japan. The most famous bit is this, which will instantly be recognizable as my own interpretation:

"Gone, gone, gone over, gone completely, then awakened, so hey! That's it!"

("Gaté, gaté, paragaté, parasamgaté. Bodhi! Svaha!")

I spun prayer wheels for the first time at

Yasaka shrine in Kyoto. That part of the heart sutra is written on the wheels, which are a horizontal row of bronze coffee-can sized (and shaped) drums on a vertical axis. Spinning a full rotation counts the same, in terms of merit-making, as saying the prayer out loud. Each time you walk around the spinning wheels you amplify their rotations, earning exponential merits.

The idea of mechanized prayer is interesting. When I was growing up, an uncle ran a small business, soon bankrupt, where people would lie on chairs that raised their arms up and down. They could take naps, the theory was, but the people would burn calories because they'd be moving their arms about. Didn't work.

Maybe that youthful experience made me skeptical of the prayer wheels. Where is the innovation barrier for prayer efficiency? Why not a conveyor belt inscribed with Sanskrit? Flip a switch and walk away. Earn merit in your sleep!

The physical connection, though, feels important. It has to be me turning the wheel. I could make a computer program that copied and pasted the Heart Sutra until the end of time, but no one would call it a blessing. But the idea of touching something, exerting effort into spinning it in the name of generating compassion, was nice.

We touch things a lot in Buddhism. Touch our hands to the prayer wheels, rub the Bodhai's belly, hold your hands on the bull statue where our own bodies hurt.

You spin the wheel because it's a new way to think about the heart sutra, which you may have theoretically read out loud thousands of times as a mantra. Kyoto is full of spectacles because the spectacle is how you reinvigorate your faith with a sense of wonder and awe again, take it out of the mundane practice that it really is.

It puts a little love in dreams back into the love in action.

FUSHIMI INARI.

Exponentials are a common theme in Kyoto. Spin the wheel while walking around the wheel and amplify your karma. At Sanjusangen-do, you can stand in front of one wall and pray to 1001 Buddhas, each one hearing and amplifying your prayer.

At the Fushimi-Inari shrine, a series of red Shinto gates lead up the side of a mountain. The gate, usually placed outside of a Shinto shrine, indicates that you are entering a space of reverence.

Fushimi-Inari is just a solid stack of fox-colored gates, suggesting an ever-amplified space of awe. The gate to awe within the gate to awe within the gate to awe, etc.

The characters written on them, which may seem like mystical wisdom to the kanji-illiterate tourist, are actually "THIS GATE BROUGHT TO YOU BY YODABASHI CAMERA!" identifying the "sponsor" of the gate.

You get tired of the awe. Then the awe comes back, and you feel inspired again, until you get distracted by the hike, and lose your awe. This happens, literally, forever.

KINKAKU-JI.

Yukio Mishima's novel, "The Temple of the Golden Pavillion," is a fictional imagining of the life of the real-life schizophrenic monk who burned the original Kinkaku-ji temple to the ground in 1950.

Mishima's monk has grown up his whole life hearing about the beauty of Kinkaku-ji, and makes a pilgrimage to see it for himself. In the book, he tells us, "I therefore staked everything not so much on the objective beauty of the temple itself as on my own power to imagine its beauty."

But love in action, warns Dostoevsky, is a harsh and dreadful thing compared to love in dreams. Our monk arrives at Kinkaku-ji and it's nothing special, a building on a lake, and somewhat small. It fails to inspire awe. In the story, the monk believes that Kinkakuji has conspired to hide its beauty from him, and longs to see its destruction.

Kinkaku-ji is disappointing. You can't go in,

for the obvious reason that a crazy monk burned it to the ground once already. It's not a 612-year-old building, it's a 62-year-old replica of 550-year-old building. It's not even the nicest temple in Kyoto.

It does, however, provide English-language fortunes for 50 yen from a bubble-gum machine. I bought one, as I do whenever I see English-language fortunes at shrines. The last time I got one it was the best possible fortune, so my checking in with the bubblegum fates at Kinkaku-ji had an air of greed to it.

Again I got the best possible fortune in all the categories, but in the matter of love – a sore subject after nights of solitary wine on the riverbanks – I was told only, "Beware of your ego."

I came to Kinkaku-ji, and Japan, and to everything in life, expecting love-in-dreams, and I've been frustrated that it has kept itself obscured and fuzzy, hiding behind the spectacular failures of my love-in-action. The Gods wrote it down on paper, in English, and sent it my way in a gumball machine; "Beware of your ego," and when I was disappointed that it didn't have more to tell me, I finally realized it was right.

In Thailand I wanted to be independent, but in Kyoto, I wanted to see my friends. Not in a needy, attached way. In a lowercase-l lonely way.

OSAKA.

I went to Osaka. The okonomiyaki in Osaka is not as good as the okonomiyaki near my house, and there is nobody to drink with. I dozed off, staring everywhere for more epiphanies, more ideas, more advice from the fox spirits. All I got was burned out neon in Blade Runner glory.

"We taught you gratitude in Thailand," said the fox, "Now we're giving you a proper sense of attachment, and we've LITERALLY spelled out your romantic troubles on a PIECE OF PAPER. What else do you want from us, man?

So hey, that's it.

28.
ON LENIN'S FEET
AND THE TAXI DRIVING BUDDHA.

If you visit Kyoto, you may stumble into a small home next door to a shrine and, as you're looking for the shrine entrance, a woman may ask you for 500 yen and assure you that there is English being spoken inside. You will go in, thinking it is a shrine, but it will not be a shrine, and the English being spoken will not be the English you paid 500 yen for.

The inside of this elderly couples' home was a ragtag assortment of Buddhist artifacts arranged like gas station memorabilia in a garage. The walls were splintered wood with some windows on a concrete floor. The host was an old man with a calm old-man voice. He would move his hands gently up and down toward the statues and speak, out of necessity, with the barest of words.

"This," he'd say, his right hand slowly descending through the air, "Cambodia."

We nodded.

"This," he'd say, his left hand an open palm gesturing toward a broken statue, "China."

We nodded. He nodded. We walked to the next room.

"Statue." It was a six-foot-tall blackened statue on the concrete floor. "Pray."

He stood in front of the statue, his fingers pointed to his eyes, then pointed to the statue's eyes. "First look, eyes." He gestured again, for emphasis. "Kneel. Heart to heart." He gestured to his heart and then to the statue's heart. Then he kneeled. "Eyes to feet." As he bowed he kept his eyes on the statue's feet.

"For good dream," he said, standing. He gestured to me with the same open hand, then to the statue.

"Pray."

So I did. My eyes matched the statue's, then my hand went from my heart to its heart, then I kneeled and looked at the feet.

I have an undisciplined mind. When I looked at the statue's feet I wasn't really looking at its feet. I had teleported to the sea-foam-green foot of the enormous reclining Buddha in Sasaguri, inscribed with golden Buddhist talismans, which visitors touch for good luck.

Then I was in the Soviet Union, contemplating the feet of Vladimir Lenin. I had seen a plaster statue of Lenin in Prague at a show of communist artifacts held in contempt by sardonic Czechs. The exhibit was in the entirely ironic Museum of Communism, advertised in posters depicting a teddy bear holding a machine gun.

Lenin's face was identical to every other portrayal of Lenin's face. This is intentional. Only certain artists could draw or sculpt those beady eyes and that pointy facial hair, always derived from his death mask or a cast of his head, so that no image would never stray from the original.

So the face of Lenin on Soviet currency was the face of Lenin hanging over school blackboards; the bust of Lenin on the piano of a party hack was the same bust in museums.

The party wanted to keep Lenin's head, like his legacy, perfect. So they went ahead and banned his deathbed warnings about Stalin, raised him to superhuman status, and controlled the way he looked in all future propaganda.

In Prague, Lenin's head was perfect. But no one seemed to care about the rest of Lenin's body until some dry-witted Czechs put the statue on the ground so we could all be taller than Lenin. There, exposed to the world, were Lenin's feet.

Instead of shoes there were giant globs of plaster. It looked like Lenin had just stepped into a foot-high pile of cow shit. I imagined the sculptor letting it go because hey, no one's going to see the shoes anyway, this thing will be on a pedestal for a million years of Communist Brotherhood, so why waste time on the feet? I imagine party officials letting it go because some day they might want to threaten the artist by exposing his neglect: "Do you even want the workers of the world to unite, comrade? I'm not so sure you do, not when your hands have sculpted feet that look... like these!"

That last thought marked the end of my meditation at the feet of a religious artifact in Kyoto. I stood and bowed, but the old man said I wasn't finished. I had to walk around to the back of the statue, he said. So I did. He showed me what to do.

"Show respect. Clear sight," he pointed to his eyes. "From front," he said, "Come to back." He pointed to his eyes again. He bowed a little. Then he said, "Takusi Duribaa desu."

This means "Taxi Driver."

"Takushi Duribaa desu ka?" I asked. ("It's taxi driver?")
"Takushi Duribaa desu," he said. ("It's taxi driver.")

I bowed. No need to be rude. From that point on he spoke entirely in very complicated Japanese except for when he tried to sell us fortunes, divided by category, for 500 yen. We passed.

I'd been thinking about Lenin's feet and Buddha as taxi driver; about the common man's work and the right path. I assumed it was a translation error, but something about paying reverence to a taxi driver artifact struck home, in a very Socialist-Republic, let-us-praise-the-common-workers sort of way.

The word he used probably wasn't katakana for Taxi Driver. It was probably something about takushiki, or clear-sightedness, maybe even takushiki-dou, "the way of clearsightedness," or Takushiki, the clear-sighted King of Sri Lankan Buddhism, who on his deathbed left us with a typically cheerful insight:

"Anyone who comes into being must decay and die. Whatever is built up, falls apart. Whatever becomes, decays. The only true happiness is in the moment when becoming and decaying are not."

"Clear-sightedness" probably doesn't involve day dreaming about Lenin stepping in dog shit when you are kneeling in a shrine. Likewise, it also probably means not pouring a bunch of plaster on Lenin's feet in the hopes that no one will notice.

We bowed to the back of the statue. I felt the same satisfaction I feel when I acknowledge the stuff hidden away in my own skull.

"Hey I'm in a new situation and I don't know what to do. I know! I'll check in with the constant stream of insecurity that has kept me company since I was nine." – *Everybody Ever*

I can bow to the loud-and-clear noise of my consciousness all day. I can watch it tell me about how I'm doing entirely awesome stuff. But when I can get at the insecurities and fear and those petty whining noises running in the background, that's when I feel like I'm really getting somewhere.

Taking this Zen thing seriously starts with making sure every side of my thoughts is worth bowing to. That's authenticity.

I can't pretend to be "OK" just because I'm getting better at hiding things from myself. I have to remember to be miserable or happy and watch myself be miserable or happy so I can get to the core of my own silly awfulness, say hello to it and then get back to being plain, pure me.

Otherwise, I'll all be caught standing up to my knees in my own bullshit when that iron curtain finally falls.

29.
ON NOT SAYING SORRY.

Lately I've embraced a daydream of an afterlife in which I finally understand what everyone else is doing. This basic fantasy found its zenith in the fleeting notion that I could simply look up everyone I knew on Wikipedia to find thorough, crowd-sourced outlines of their internal machinations; this was compounded by the dream that Jonathan Franzen would write all the entries.

Even among people who use the same words for feelings and ideas, life is a never-ending series of confusing propositions and clumsy negotiations, but try living without it. Learning to tolerate all that ambiguity is one of the reasons I went abroad: To see where I start and years of living in the English-speaking enclave of American culture ends.

Ms. Kuroguchi was put in charge of making sure I didn't die, which would have been inconvenient for my office. She was thorough, but spoke in a distinctly Japanese math. Everything was parenthetical and algebraic. Nothing was straightforward, variables were constantly implied. My work schedule would be evoked rather than explained. The Japanese call it "reading the air," a skill that English would best translate as "read her mind."

Once, she scolded me for arriving at 8:29 for my 8:30 workday, insisting that "other teachers know where you live, so you have no excuse."

One day she suggested that "perhaps" the English Club students would meet me at 4:15, but that "maybe" they had a study group, "I can't be sure." One student might, *perhaps*, come to computer room C, but perhaps now computer room C is locked for repairs, so they will use computer room B? "I'm not sure about that," she said, "but maybe it's the case, so, we don't know when the students will come."

"OK," I said, desperately reducing her stream of fractions; "Can you unlock the security alarm so I can wait for them?" She said sure. She didn't do it, so I tripped the alarm at 4:15. She ran upstairs and, shouting in front of students, said that she told me to talk to her before coming here. "I TOLD YOU THAT."

I, for the first time, and to the cheering of students, shouted back at her and flung my hands in the air dismissively. I went downstairs and submitted my contracting papers for dramatic flair, refusing to renew – effectively canceling my life in Japan. I'd planned to do it anyway. It just felt more satisfying this way.

This mildly inflamed exchange would go unnoticed in America, where this is how you order breakfast on a busy day. But here, two teachers shouting at each other is blockbuster office gossip.

She didn't speak to me for a week, which is a common approach to conflict resolution among many people here. Typically, you just avoid conflict at all costs. If someone seems to be sparking conflict – in this case, me – you avoid them. I've screwed up paperwork and felt like shaving my head to drive away the cold stares of co-workers who don't say a word, but then again, they don't say a word to me, anyway.

In the case of the dramatic doorway, staff members eventually held an intervention. I was told I was "one percent responsible" – after all, I did open a secured door without checking. Also, she was older, so I had to apologize. By this face-saving logic, the shop keeper may have been robbed, but maybe he owes the burglar a tiny apology for leaving all that money in his store?

This "1 percent responsible" line was told to me casually at first and then in a sit-down meeting in the conference room. I should apologize, save the wa, and complete my transformation into Japanese office culture, or I could be American.

"No," I said. "I'm not doing that."

"But she will not speak with you unless you apologize to her."

"Well," I said, "That sounds wonderful."

OK. I'm petty.

If I'm going to expect empathy from other people, then it's only honest to extend empathy toward them, and yet, I'm failing here. Someone who has never transitioned into another culture can't really relate to my experience. I know that. And I'm not angry about that. If she can't communicate with me, she can't imagine how confusing everything is. It's quite simple for her to assume that so much more of her understanding is also part of my frame of reference. She can't see that the heightened awareness of my surroundings carries a unique form of mental exhaustion.

But I just can't bring myself to apologize to her, especially not because she's older and so I must have been the one who made the mistake. That's just not a part of this culture I am willing to take on. And that feels uncomfortable!

After all, shouldn't I be judging my actions in this situation by the context that everyone I work with sees it – that there's no harm in apologizing, that there's no shame, and even a bit of strength, in taking the hit to my ego to save everyone in the office some tension?

It's tough, explaining this to unsympathetic observers. I know I'm supposed to empathize with those who can't empathize with me. But I make dozens of exhausting concessions every day, themselves becoming an added source of mental stress.

Refusing to apologize for losing my temper to an unsympathetic office tyrant was my one stand against the thousands of tiny stresses that have chiseled into my skin like fiberglass. I had to draw the line somewhere and make a stand for my idea of who I am, instead of getting lost into what I see as humiliating acquiescence. Sometimes, you gotta not assimilate.

Someday, perhaps we'll end up in some enveloping consciousness where we can understand everything anyone has ever done with absolute empathy and forgiveness. The daydream starts with my resident office tyrant, Ms. Kuroguchi, understanding how different my life here is from what I am used to; it extends outward to people I've loved who didn't believe me when I told the truth. It extends to people who have suffered from my lack of courage, selfishness, ego or anger.

This fantasy is also my chance to understand the mystery of other people. It's easy to assume we all act on the same impulses, desires, and sense of what's right. But then you come abroad, and you realize there are a million ways for good intentions to manifest themselves. Maybe the source of all pain in a good-intentioned world is not articulating our intentions properly.

I want to cultivate empathy. I want to give people the benefit of the doubt, assume that everyone has had their own reasons for doing the things they have done, to understand not only why people have hurt me but the extent to which I have hurt people. And then I wonder, if my vision of a perfect afterlife is just one giant cluster of mutual understanding, am I doing enough to cultivate it while I'm still alive?

I don't know, but I never did apologize. And six months later, I went home.

30.
ON AWKWARD ACTS OF GENEROSITY.

It should have been a yes or no question. It was exam day for high schools in my prefecture, and teachers were forbidden to leave the building, lest they pass on crucial details of the test to the legion of spies waiting outside.

The schools offered a bento (lunch box) delivery to the office for 600 yen. The test is a two-day operation: The exam, then the grading. I decided to buy one for exam day and pack a lunch for grading day to save money, but a teacher, Mr. Tanagawa, secretly paid for my bento. When the bentos arrived, I went to pay.

"You don't have to pay," he explained, "because I already paid for it."

Thanks!

***

It was raining the next day. When the bentos arrived, I'd forgotten both my umbrella and my packed lunch. I scraped some coins together from my desk and prepared for the rainy walk to the corner convenience store for a salad and ham sandwich. But first, I'd ask about the bento situation.

In an American office where there's a planned delivery, someone might say, "Hey, are there any extra sandwiches? I'll pitch in if there are." Maybe someone ordered one and forgot or something. The answer might be something like, "No, everyone took their sandwich." End of the story.

Here's what happens when you ask if there's an extra lunch in Japan. I asked my new supervisor – Ms. Kuroguchi had been reassigned – "I don't have a bento today, right?"

This was recklessly casual and loaded. As those words left my mouth, I knew I had lost control. My new supervisor instantly stood up from her desk where she'd been eating.

"You told me you didn't want *bento* today."
"I know. I'm just making sure."
"Do you want bento?"
"No, no, I'm just seeing, I looked at the paper and there's no line through my name, so I'm confused."
"But you said no bento today."

First off, let me explain what's happened, on a couple of levels. First, asking "I don't have a bento today, right?" translates, in that hint-at-everything manner of Japanese communication, that maybe probably I was expecting bento.

Second, "just making sure" doesn't qualify that assumption at all. It continues to imply that there was some expectation of having a bento. My reason for this assumption was the off chance that, last week, when I'd ordered it, I'd actually gone ahead and ordered two. I also thought that, when my co-worker paid for the bento I'd ordered, he might have paid for it on a day that I said I'd bring my lunch.

Rather than stopping at "No, that's right, you didn't order a bento," my supervisor gave her famous last words, "wait a minute," and went to the desk of the next person in the hierarchy, the woman who ordered and distributed the bentos.

This woman went to the school's central office and returned with a list of bento orders, which seemed to be bound together and preserved in a book. Next to my name was a circle for day 1, and no circle for day 2.

"So," they said, "You didn't order the bento." "I know," I said. "That's fine. Thanks so much!"

Then the plot thickened.

"But there is one extra bento." She asked if I'd want the extra bento. I said sure, thinking this would be easy. "But you said you wanted to take the convenience store lunch," she said.

"Yes. That's fine, I'll do that, but it's raining, so if I don't have to walk to the convenience store, I'd take the extra bento."

"Wait a minute."

My supervisor and the office secretary looked through the list of who ordered bento and did a mental count of everyone in the room who was eating one. She ran to a teacher sitting at a table and said something in Japanese. This teacher stood up, walked over to me and the secretary, and they all spoke in a frenzy of Japanese, too fast for me to catch.

The new teacher walked over to his desk, came up to me, and offered me his home-made boxed lunch.

"Please, have his lunch," my supervisor told me.
"Oh," I said. "No, no, it's OK, I don't want someone else's lunch. I'll just go get my lunch at the convenience store as I planned."
"But, you told me you don't want to go to the conbini."
"If there's an extra bento, I'll take it," I said, "but I don't want to take away someone's lunch or dinner!" The three teachers talked. My supervisor turned to me again. "Wait a minute."

The three teachers counted the names on the sign-up sheet for bento and then counted the bentos in the delivery box, checking it against the number of bentos listed on the receipt.

"I'm so sorry," my supervisor said. "There is no extra bento."
"That's absolutely fine," I said. "I'll just go to the convenience store."
"Did you order the bento?"
"No, I was just confused, because yesterday

Mr. Tanagawa paid for my lunch, so I didn't know if I ordered it yesterday or today."
"You had the lunch order paid for by Mr. Tanagawa?"
"Yesterday."
"But today you don't want the bento?"
"Yes. It's OK. It's perfect. *Everything is perfect.*"

I went to the convenience store on the corner and bought a ham sandwich, a salad and some milk tea. When I came back, Mr. Tanagawa asked me to eat lunch with him.

"You shouldn't tell other teachers I paid for your lunch," he said. "I could get into trouble."
"Oh," I said. "I'm sorry. I didn't know."
"It's OK, but it can cause many kinds of problems for me."
"Oh, wow, well, you're very kind! I'm sorry, I didn't know."

"Now, I also must apologize to you, because I caused so much confusion for you today."

"No, no. I didn't have any confusion at all. I just checked to see if there was an extra bento. You were very kind to pay for it! It was not necessary at all."

"No no, it's my pleasure. But I caused a lot of trouble for the other teachers, so I am very sorry that I troubled you."

In the midst of that exchange, the teacher who'd offered me his homemade lunch looked at my bag of convenience store sandwich, groaned in Japanese, shook his head and walked away.

"Why did you refuse his lunch?" Mr. Tanagawa asked.

"I didn't want to take his homemade lunch from him!"

"But it's very rude to refuse him. He is an older teacher. He is a very kind teacher, and you said no, it's a kind of insult, maybe." He thought for a minute. "You didn't understand he wanted you to eat the lunch, maybe? Right?"

He leaned in on "right" as if to say, "you'll go along with this story, right?"
I didn't catch on at first. He looked annoyed. He emphasized the sentence again.
"You didn't understand he was offering you his lunch. RIGHT?"
"OK," I said. "Right."
"Wait a minute."

Mr. Tanagawa came back with the teacher who'd offered me lunch and said something in Japanese. The other teacher nodded and said, "OK."

Mr. Tanagawa explained. "I told him you didn't understand."

Japan presents a tangled web of reciprocity in its daily acts of kindness. These result in obligations that I've found overwhelming: I prefer not to be obligated to anybody, but in Japan, it can be insulting to refuse an

171

obligation to another person. Refusing an act of kindness – like taking that teacher's lunch – is a refusal to give back a future kindness. Refusing any kind of favor risks coming across as declaring, "Don't do me any favors!"

It's clear in the enkai tradition of pouring drinks for everyone around you, and never refusing when someone offers you a drink. You can think of this drinking party as a metaphor for social contracts in Japan: You accept a drink from your neighbor and agree to pour a drink for your neighbor. Refuse the drink and you refuse the obligation to serve it later. Drawn to its logical end, you end up with a very dull office party.

There are daily gifts and favors that draw you into the social web. I find these threatening, not reassuring. They impose on my independence – creating debts I'll have to repay in unpredictable ways, at inconvenient times, when the person offering a favor has complete control over what's being presented to me. It feels like a trap.

But there's also the shame of being asked to return a favor I can't possibly repay. Obligations are especially threatening when you don't know what those return favors might be, especially when what seems like an even exchange of favors between two Japanese natives might be wildly disproportionate when redeemed from an illiterate foreigner.

There have been many acts of kindness in

Japan that have gone so far overboard that they began to make me nervous, more than appreciative, which has spawned a bit of soul-searching throughout the years I've been here. In Japan, this is called "arigata meiwaku," an unwanted kindness, usually presented to butter someone up for a favor.

**

Once, a friend from America visited and picked up a 100-yen coin that an older woman dropped on the train platform. The woman asked where we were going in broken English.

She lead us to the train, which was kind enough. She then boarded the train, rode it with us for twenty minutes, took us to a shop in the city we were going to, bought us a snack, lead us to a temple, and then took us to the museum, where she arranged to have an English guide give us a tour.

The problem is, this is all remarkably kind; but it also wasn't anything that I had asked for. I felt guilty talking to my friend in English when the woman didn't speak English. At a certain point we actually tried to lose her by thanking her and ducking into a shop; when we left the shop she was there, waiting for us.

A similar thing happened in Kyoto. We were looking for the subway line to our hostel, which wouldn't have been difficult, but the moment we looked at the map a man came over to us, told us where to go and lead us to the train platform. We thanked him.

He got on the train with us, rode it to the station where we needed to transfer and showed us the transfer train. We thanked him. He waited until the train arrived and got on the transfer train. Once we got off the train at our stop, he walked up the stairs with us to the exit of the train station.

We asked if he was going to our neighborhood. He shook his head. No, he said, he was going to Osaka.

He bowed and we bowed back at him; there was nothing we could do to pay him back for going an hour out of his way on a work night to show us how to get to a hostel we honestly could have come to by ourselves.

It feels terrible to complain about the excessive kindness of friends and strangers. I think the guilt it inspires causes a lot of people to seek a less benevolent explanation – that perhaps foreigners are treated like children, those feelings of looming obligation sublimated into the rejection of our coddling. I can't speak to the motivations of the Japanese people who have acted kindly to the point of awkwardness, I can only speak for me.

I like my debts paid in full, and I want to know the repayment terms before I agree to anything. This is probably the result of being raised in a relatively independent culture, where the reigning fantasies of film and song are odes to severing ties and breaking free of our duties, not relishing them. We see a web of interconnected obligations as a source of deprivation, something that holds us back, not something that supports us in a safety net of mutual responsibility.

Americans are inherently selfish, some drunk Japanese people tell me. "Not you," they say. "The culture." I used to argue that our ideas of selfishness and social good were just more centered to individual freedoms, but this makes no sense here. The American Dream, this notion of "liberty," isn't a global dream. It's a culturally constructed one. It is too obvious to say, but not all people long to be "free" in the American sense because not everyone wants to do things "the American way."

And that's fine. But I value my independence, and I am constantly fighting to protect it from staggering acts of kindness and generosity – the American dream.

31.
ON INVENTING YOURSELF
IN JAPAN.

Living in Japan is living in a thought experiment.

What if you could take away the institutional cues from your environment – your idea of a hospital vs a clinic, for example; the idea of what policemen do, or the role of teachers. Strip away the idea of how you achieve wealth and success. Next, remove and rearrange social cues: The train becomes a quiet place for resting. Your superiors are the people older than you, not necessarily the hardest working or most qualified.

Because the institutions have changed, so have the people around you. Society is organized differently, so accomplishment requires a different set of skills. Different definitions of accomplishment lead to different tactics for reaching goals. The culture praises traits that help them meet that different set of goals; they don't value the traits that helped you achieve goals back home.

In fact, many of your positive traits will become incomprehensible. I was born in a culture that values efficiency. I came into a culture that values perseverance. Long attention spans are praised here, patience is expected. I'm lazy and scatterbrained. It doesn't help.

So what else happens? How do you start reacting to this new environment? Perhaps it's a bad sign that after reading about monkeys, my mind wandered to my life as an expat. But a study, published in the April 2013 issue of the journal *Science,* made me think about social adaptation.

In the experiment, researchers dyed two batches of corn – one pink, one blue. For two groups of monkeys, the blue corn was soaked in a disgusting liquid, and the pink stuff was standard monkey corn. For the other groups of monkeys, they switched it.

So, two groups of monkeys grew accustomed to pink being inedible, two grew accustomed to blue being inedible. Soon enough, the monkeys only ate one color of corn (the delicious one).

Then the scientists stopped making the other color taste so bad. Once the monkeys got used to which color was good, they both ended up being the same. What happened was interesting: High-status monkeys never bothered eating the gross-colored corn, but low-status monkeys occasionally had to. And even though these low-status monkeys knew that the corn was identical to the good stuff (identical, now, aside from the color), they still favored the "good" color when they could get it. Meanwhile, babies who grew up watching mom eat one color of corn barely even registered that the other color of corn was even food. They'd shit in it.

Monkeys shitting in food have a lot in common with me, as an expat. I'm not always down on my life, of course, but anyone in one culture can get accustomed to interacting with certain things in certain ways. It's a given: The institutions shape how we interact with them, and then that shapes how we interact with each other. Sometimes this institution is a school or job hunt, and sometimes it's the people giving us corn.

But then the researchers did something really cool. They took some monkeys and introduced them to the monkeys in other areas – areas where the opposite color of corn was "the good stuff."

Wild Vervet monkeys, trained to eat only pink-dyed or blue-dyed corn and shun the other color, quickly began eating the disliked-color corn when they moved from a pink-preferred setting to a blue-is-best place, and vice versa.

These guys went in, looked around, and lost their old cultural identities. This is, at a literally primal level, a version of culture shock. Humans, lucky us, have a much more complicated set of adaptations to deal with. We don't just want to eat some corn, we want our identities validated.

The different ways things are done in a different culture causes people to value different things and to express them differently — to the demands of different environments and institutions. So while in America I'm praised for my directness and efficiency, in Japan, that stuff just isn't as valuable.

Stripped of the stuff I've always thought I was good at, I start to panic. It's like I'm a vervet who was really good at finding pink corn scattered across the brush, and now here I am, being told that everyone wants the blue stuff.

Some of the youngins don't even know you can eat the pink stuff! The imaginative capacity of the people around you is built around fundamental assumptions reinforced by institutional arrangements. The head boss wants blue, so blue's valuable.

You enter school and must adapt to the school; you enter work and must adapt to the office. Your parents worked in a particular way, so you expect your children to work that way. Even when you leave these environments, a lot of the adaptations stick around.

We're often forced, through lack of imagination, into applying our background to a new place where our ways of doing stuff may not actually work or be wanted. It's what every human being does, everywhere, when confronted with the unknown: We try to relate to it using what we know.

You're expected to show up to work 10 minutes before the work day so you can sit in your desk and wait for the bell that starts your work day. It sounds insane, but you do it, because that is what your job values. Before long, even though you know it's ridiculous, you might find yourself feeling slightly resentful of anyone who comes into work after you – even when they're still early. You start watching, observing, and then adopting the culture. Which might be fine and good. Except that it might also, eventually, spark an identity crisis.

One of the really nice things about humans is that we are children for a really, really long time. That means we get the benefits of safely playing in the world before embarking on it "for real." Human evolution has been driven by the imaginative capacity of children, because it prepares us not only for the tasks that we will, inevitably, set out to do, but also prepares us for a wide range of wildly abstract tasks that we may never need to solve.

Imagination as adults molds itself to the problems that need solving. When adult imagination is applied to a problem that doesn't need solving, we just end up calling it art.

So the thought experiment: Placed into a new culture, with new demands that reward new traits, how do you decide your definition of you, and what part of you is your imagination that's been molded to the institutions you grew up in? With these institutions gone, how much of you do you know is really you? How do you decide what habits to cull and which to hold on to?

Adaptation eases the social pressure, of course, but the endless series of social and professional expectations can have a draining effect on the agency and free will that most Americans call their "selves." It's an identity crisis! I, for one, began to resent the endless stream of unexplained changes I was starting to make.

Initially I embraced adaptation, priding myself on not walking while drinking soda, then finding myself panicking, too far on the other side of the line, when I'd realized how miserable I was feeling under the weight of thousands of daily compromises. I slowly climbed back to myself, but always careful to stay within the boundaries of my adopted culture.

Fundamentally, of course, showing up to work early; never expressing my objections to decisions of superiors; asking the permission of multiple people to do simple tasks, such as going to the bank on my lunch break; submitting my holiday itinerary to the evaluation of office managers, etc – these are not expressions of my "true spirit or nature," nor are they intended to be humiliating.

They're merely a conflict between what my home institutions have taught me is valuable – free agency, independence, critical thinking – and what my new institutions feel are valuable – group-orientation, respect to hierarchy, selflessness. The tension between these cultures manifests in the constant batting down of your personal expression. In America, this expression is what makes you yourself.

One's true self, though, probably isn't found by shuffling between the conflicting expectations of the institutions you were born in and the ones you work under.

Even the rebellions are shaped by the institutions. When I took a trip to Korea, I was tired of the rigamarole of seeking permission for international travel. Instead of submitting my itinerary, I submitted a vacation plan that listed five days in a city 20 minutes away and submitted it to my school. They had no idea why I would be staying 20 minutes away for five days but stamped their approval.

I saw it as striking a major blow of victory for my independence of spirit. An insurrection against paperwork and bureaucracy. Nobody tells me what to do!

That rebellion, of course, was shaped by the institution I rebelled against. So, was it really me?

Cantankerous independence is on that national checklist of American traits, after all. It's unlikely that I would have found myself taking pride in fudging the truth on a piece of paperwork in any other context.

This is the deeper level of the thought experiment.

You're in this new society and you are bringing habits from the old, and you are tasked with finding "yourself," theoretically, something that exists independent of those two extremes. Some celebrate their home culture, or find pride in their nationality for the first time; Texans start carrying around rodeo lassos, Englishmen start wearing bowler hats.

There's no shame in this, of course. Stepping outside of your culture can reveal it from a distance, giving you insight into what makes your culture unique. Once you expand your imaginative capacity to a new set of problems abroad, you can start appreciating the elegance of the solutions at home.

But where are *you*?

To answer this question we have to go back to an idea I mentioned earlier: When imagination is applied to a problem that doesn't need solving, you end up with art.

Art may be too loaded a word. Watch kids in a park, they're doing the same thing. Hanging out, making stuff to do, inventing games, applying all sorts of unproductive imagination. Art and play are the raw manifestations of ourselves, often, though not always, free of the constraints of the institutions we're supported by.

Art and play have rules, but they're just contained to make sure we enjoy the game. We can enjoy leisure because the intention is only the pleasure of being ourselves. We invent ways to kill time.

Of course, institutions are man-made. We invented them to solve collective problems and societies organized themselves around the best ideas.

Expats – even those who travel for a short time – are required to expand their imaginative capacity, because they are required to navigate an entirely new set of institutional constraints. If we apply ourselves to imagining new solutions, we're expanding our ideas about what is possible.

Rather than become constrained to the social or institutional conventions of home, and rather than rebelling against them, we can invent our own possibilities, interpretations, solutions and work-arounds, shift our definitions.

We don't have to define ourselves by reactions to everything – especially when we're stuck helplessly applying our old ways of working to a new situation. We can tap on our inner capacity for invention. We can approach it as helpless children, or we can embrace it – as helpless children.

Perhaps it is clumsy and stressful, and easier to tweak our existing recipes to work for a new palate. But there is a lot to be said for finding a "third way" aside from rebelling and acquiescing You can build your own alternative, try to see things from a new set of eyes, play around as you try to figure out what works.

Taken as a game – as a form of play, or even a creative process – this invention of ourselves requires an openness to extreme uncertainty. That's hard. Anxiety will rise naturally from any search for resolution and certainty. The trick is letting go of that need. I always imagined that the stakes in Japan were really high, that this uncertainty could be eradicated through "knowing." This is perfectly healthy – it inspired me to learn the language, study the customs, etc. But knowing only took me so far.

If it's a game, then not knowing isn't so bad. Uncertainty isn't a failure to adapt. It just means there's no routine yet – that we've stumbled into a gap between what we thought we should do in our "real life" and the unknown expectations of our new life. Uncertainty doesn't always have to be a failure; it's an invitation to invent a new routine.

Maybe it means becoming more tolerant or accepting. Maybe it means saying "yes" more often, or "no." You can make the game, simply, to stop freaking out about the uncertainty. Don't worry if you slip up; it's just a game, the rules are being made up, and nothing serious is at stake. You aren't going to go crazy, it just feels that way. Let go of certainty, and you'll be fine.

When imagination is applied to a problem that doesn't need solving, you end up inventing yourself.

32.
ON MEETING THE STRAWBERRY.

Before I came to Japan, I told myself that this was a bit of practice for dying. It wasn't the most upbeat assessment of moving abroad, but it rang true. I was about to end my life, or at least, I was about to take a practice round for facing the real challenge, when that once uncountable expanse of unspent days becomes a precious commodity.

I left for Japan to practice losing my ties to things. While a punching bag doesn't prepare you for a street fight, and target practice doesn't prepare you for war, we might hope that practice makes it more familiar, and easier to face the real struggle when it comes.

With some maudlin exceptions, everything living seems to prefer it to dying. The battle I've had with my ego while abroad has humbled me about that final interview with eternity. I liked who I was in America. I liked my friends and family, my job, my stuff. I liked *me*. But I initiated the rituals of departure: the countdown of the-last-time-I'll-do-its, final goodbyes before a solitary, tear-filled taxi ride as the sun rose over Logan airport.

People told me they'd never do what I was doing because they'd be too sad. Crying seems like a bad reason to avoid something, but boy, humans sure do a lot to avoid it. I always feel sad about goodbyes, perhaps because of the practice rule: The sadness of a goodbye is practice for all future goodbyes and all final sadnesses, and who wants to think about that?

When you are a healthy sad about the ending of something, you connect to the ending of everything.

***

In Japan, my identity decomposed into new soil. I struggled to hold on to what I was. Panic attacks and anxiety were warnings that my identity – the one I liked, the one I was quite fond of, the one that spent years figuring out how to get what it wanted – was being replaced by a new set of adaptations that were radically changing who I was. I wasn't losing my mind, I was losing my ego.

The ego, in the Buddhist sense, is the part of your inner dialogue that makes it all about you. It isn't arrogant, per se, just preoccupied with itself. Some people walk into a room and feel like everyone's been waiting for them, some people walk into a room and feel like everyone is criticizing them. The ego is the thing that tells you that *you* are the one being noticed and responded to.

As the guardian of my shifting selfhood, my ego was anxious. It placed extraordinary value on the position of my "identity," a pebble mistaken for a boulder submerged into rushing waters. I wanted the water to divert itself around a pebble, but water always wins.

I walked through a cave in Yamaguchi recently, stones full of holes caused by tiny drops of water from the ceiling, accumulated over thousands of years. Nothing is impenetrable.

I spent too much time in Japan fighting a process that made me, in the end, more sane, simple, tolerant and yielding.

My ego hasn't shut up. It's still there, starting sentences with "Me / My / I" and using words like "deserve" and "should," the fighting words of a toddler, the battle cry of everything bitter. "My coworkers should help me with moving," it says. "My employer should be paying the costs of closing this apartment." All completely unreasonable, all about me, me, me.

Lately when I hear myself complaining I ask my ego to call me back once it's calmed down, so we can have a rational conversation. It's a drunk party guest. We can't argue because it just raises its voice, so we agree to disagree and I move on to another internal conversation. But I can't kick it out, either. Sometimes it says something useful, like "Look buddy, maybe you shouldn't give away everything you own." Or, "Don't give up this part of who you are, just to make your boss happy."

The "I/Me/Mine" stream has its uses, because hey, I have to survive. I'm no monk. I'm trying to approach my ego as an advice columnist and not my superior officer.

***

What seemed to happen in my last weeks in Japan is that rather than feeling a sense of attachment and a longing to stay, I had already left.

Some students gave me a basket of flowers. They're plastic so I don't have to water them. It's a nice gesture, but preparing to leave, I felt like I was those plastic flowers, being there and looking the part but not really living.

Japan is already a memory. What was at times a panic-inducing environment feels like vapor instead of a torrential stream. I've learned to cope, now I'm going to leave. Rather than being sad about another departure, my ego is keeping a grudge. Japan wasn't kind to it, seemed to act ambivalent to its existence. How dare you, Japan! So my ego responds with all the intelligence of a "rubber and glue" joke: "Hey Japan! You ignored me for so long, acted like I wasn't real, well guess what? *You're* not real."

What a bore. The ego troll spent years complaining about all the injustices it had to endure, and now that we're leaving, it's acting like it was no big deal.

The inner troll doesn't want to feel myself leaving, because I'd be reduced to a bubbling puddle of tears. It doesn't want me to feel that healthy sadness of a goodbye. Saying goodbye to anything is saying goodbye to everything. It's terrified of letting go, terrified of anything that doesn't have itself at the center.

***

I remember thinking, a week before my flight home, that I should probably cry or something, but I was on perpetual guard duty, distancing myself instead. I found myself scrunching up my face in bed at night, giving myself a headache to stave off tears. It's not like anyone can even see me.

I just really hate crying.

A Haiku by Issa:

The trout, looking up:
"Just be brave, cherry blossom,
Brave enough to fall."

***

Friends who have left Japan give me the impression that the country eventually slips away into a hallucinatory blur, like grainy film footage that gets worn down when you replay it. Internal movies, bubbling from the heat of internal projection, losing focus, filled with the stories you tell instead of the things that happened.

I believe this, because memory isn't real. Without the "permanent" backbone of memories – the buildings, the faces of people, the train routes and the daily kanji practice that create a concrete reminder of past experiences with those buildings, faces or flashcards – there's nothing to hang those memories on.

Photographs, journals: Water rushes over everything. The life beyond the Instagram border. Memory is just the polite word for imagination. You start photocopying the photocopy of a bad drawing you never actually made. I wanted to soak up all the realness of Japan while I was in it, but I couldn't.

***

For a long time I loved the phrase *ichi-go ichi-e* because I thought it meant "meeting a strawberry." Literally, it is "one life, one meeting," the meeting being a person or a challenge, or, as I like to think, meeting one strawberry.

Ichi-go ichi-e is best understood if we retroactively apply it to the bushido days, when a warrior would train with as much intensity as a real battle. If he fell off his horse and injured his arm, he would get back on the horse, carrying on instead of restarting, because he does not believe in the idea of "trying again." Each move should be completed as if it were his only chance. He would imagine practice as if it were real life, or else it wasn't really practice, just play-acting.

When things were hard, I would tell myself, "this is practice" as a way of separating myself from the pain of real emotions. The correct technique, perhaps, is to feel those experiences completely, to let the tears flow, to live through it without going numb. To practice feeling things fully, instead of practicing detachment to them. It means a detachment from yourself: Detaching from what gets in the way of living.

You will never do anything "again." You only eat one strawberry, even when you are eating a bucket of strawberries. I should practice remembering that, practice experiencing my life fully while it is happening. *Meeting the Strawberry*, rather than eating one after the other until they all become a mash.

Everything is practice, nothing is practice. We prepare for the real thing by living it.

Issa:

This world of dew
is only a world of dew.
And yet...

INDEX 1.
IDEAS THAT MIGHT HELP OUT.

I have a few months left before starting my new life in London, but I've already filled 11 rubbish bags to bursting with the debris of my life in Japan.

Nothing can stay, and the lack of sentimentality I'm forced to feign has only made me more nostalgic.

Rummaging through the closets, I see myself as I was a year ago, two years ago, three years ago, an archaeological dig through handkerchiefs and exotic (spicy citrus!) Kit-Kats I was supposed to mail home in 2010.

Throwing it away feels like erasing a well-earned scar. This was my stuff – these are the remnants of experiences that defined me here. Sending it all out to the bins means it isn't around to facilitate nostalgia or reflection.

So I've decided to write a few things down – notes, I guess, for the next person who might take over this apartment, my job, and my life.

These ideas have kept me sane – or have been learned after losing and finding that sanity – as I spent time in Japan practicing to become the person I am today.

COMPLAIN ON TUESDAYS.

Complaining is useful to a point. It's important to feel supported, especially if your problems make you feel isolated and alone. Complaining is a comforting indulgence, like chocolate, and too much makes it hard to want anything else. Chocolate complaints on the ends of your fingertips will end up smeared on everything you touch.

You will feel a lot of emotions that will inspire you to complain about your life. Frustration, loneliness, a sense of constant confusion. These are natural to feel and they are natural to talk about. Talk about them on Tuesday – or any one night of the week where you can go out, get a beer and eat all the chocolate you want. The rest of the week, talk about ideas, projects and the things you can control.

EVERYBODY IS A COUNTRY.

If you have ever been to a "culture festival," you might have felt the sense, as I have, that there was something missing from the picture being painted by ceremonial dances and $1 samples of national cuisine. The idea that a culture can be reduced to music and food preferences is revealed as a total absurdity the moment you encounter your own country at one of these events. Country music and hot dogs – now, you know about

America!

While the culture of a country is awkward to define by its music and food, so, too, is a human being.

Music – and culture, like art and movies and books – was how I defined myself in America, how I made friends and influenced people. But this is more or less presenting a "cultural festival" version of anyone's identity.

Here, in Japan, people don't always react the way I would to things. The idea of defining my friendship circle by the music people listen to, the books people have read, or the movies they like now strikes me as insanely superficial. I'm proud to say that most of my best friends have absolutely no interest in anything I like – and I've found that, in the absence of going along with pretense, I've gotten totally sick of a lot of what I used to like.

Culture is more complicated than that, and so are friends. You don't get much sense of how different a country will be – the subtle changes in approach, soft shifts in the way people interpret you and your actions – until you really live there, really get to know it. Friendships are the same. Sometimes people withdraw in a situation where I might reach out. Sometimes people are embarrassed by things that I'd be proud of. Everybody is a different country! Our parents, schooling, friendships, life experiences, all give us a different idea of how to be with other people, how to share ourselves, how to set and realize our goals – even if we grew up across the street.

My most inspiring friendships here have been with people I fear I might have ignored back home because we didn't like the same bands. Don't judge a country by its food stall.

IF A FRIENDSHIP MAKES YOU ANXIOUS, IT'S NOT A FRIENDSHIP.

People are strange, and perhaps that is amplified by the constant state of stress I'm under as an expat. For my first few years I found most other expats incomprehensible. I'd get angry. People were abrasive, shifty. It seems like nobody takes anybody else very seriously at all.

If everybody is a foreign country, not every country is a place you'd actually want to live. You don't have to. We wouldn't move to a country simply because it's there, and we shouldn't be friends using that criteria, either. But when it comes to the limited pool of expat friends you can make here, you go with what's there — at least until you break the barrier of local friendships.

Stressful countries might offer rewards and experiences you could never find anywhere else. You might see pictures and be filled with a yearning to conquer the challenges it presents to you. That is an enriching compulsion for travel, and a terrible compulsion for relationships. Some people are not good for you. When it comes to countries, go for the hard ones. When it comes to friends, stick to the comforting ones.

YOU CAN BE ALONE.

Loneliness is kind of the prevailing story of the expat life. It's the underlying state that propels people to traveling adventures, to hostel hookups and to Instagramming every meal. Sometimes, even at home, it felt like there was just no point in doing anything unless someone was there to share it with. We are all social beings who like to have a chat now and then, but requiring the presence of others is a textbook case of neediness.

For a short time, I rejected my neediness. I traveled by myself to Thailand and Kyoto. It wasn't the first time I'd traveled entirely solo, but it was reassuring to survive in a foreign country without anything but my own resourcefulness. I have friends who feel alone, and it makes them sad, and this is human. But it is important to know that you can do things without a companion.

YOU DON'T HAVE TO BE ALONE.

Isolation is not ideal, either. For a long time, I was obsessed with the idea that I should never need anything outside of myself. I wanted to cultivate detachment. To a point, this is useful. But it's OK to care about people, to get dragged into feeling things, even unpleasant things. That's part of life. Isolating yourself from the pain of human drama is impossible, but indulging in it is unnecessary. Care about people, even if it hurts sometimes, and never be ashamed of wanting good company.

YOU DON'T HAVE TO HAVE FUN.

Fun, I've realized, is a side effect, not a goal. Life requires rest, security, and the comfort of people who actually care about you. When those conditions are met, happiness organically emerges. It takes time to get that all in place, and it can be frustrating here, as the connections you make are, by nature, fleeting. Don't depend on forcing "fun" into a substitute for the things you actually need.

YOU CAN LEAVE.

At every peak and crest of the culture shock wave you're jostled about. The train conductor won't refund your ticket and you can't understand why, your coworkers give you mutually exclusive instructions on what to do (and then tell you to do both), you go to the grocery store and have no idea where to find a sponge and you assume that's why you feel like crying beside the bath soap.

You will feel powerless, but there is always something you can control. I found it in my legs and in my writing. I threw dinner parties. Some people pick up an instrument, some learn to cook or to mix an excellent martini. But I've learned a fundamental truth: I can always leave. We can say no. You can quit your job. You can break up with your partner. You can call off the wedding. You don't have to go to that party you're dreading. It doesn't make you a failure.

I always worry that saying no came from being uncomfortable, that I was scared of an experience, that somehow I wouldn't grow as a person if I didn't stick it through. Might be true, might not be. But you always have the option to cancel. Likewise, once you remember that you can leave, you have the choice to stay. That choice is surprisingly powerful.

YOU CAN CHANGE.

A lot of things change in two and a half years, and the transient habits that I trust to stay with me have proven to be unreliable. The mannerisms, ways of talking, the way my laugh sounds – have all changed, and for a short time at home, sitting in my childhood bedroom, it became confusing to think about which parts of me were the real me, the permanent me, and which parts would be replaced to serve some future need.

Human personalities are disconcertingly malleable, and we have a tendency to be snobby about short-term adaptations. We view them as growth because they make us happier in whatever situation we find ourselves in. But this may be a bit of self-flattery.

We may, in fact, not be "growing," but merely changing ourselves to adapt to short-term circumstances; to make life a little easier to live.

Maybe this sounds like a let-down. I'm casting doubts on the happy myth of personal growth. But I think that this is also kind of beautiful. We take what we can of the world and work it into the broader composition of our lives. We become new, and we become something that makes us happier than where we began.

We travel to grow, and then we fight change every day. We panic that we're losing our selves, when that's what growth is supposed to do: You've grown. The old you is going to appear smaller. Don't be frightened.

THE AUTHOR.

Eryk Salvaggio was an American newspaper editor in Bangor, Maine before teaching English in Japan with the JET Programme. He lived in Fukuoka City from 2010-2013, writing a blog, *This Japanese Life*, about Japanese culture and the tiny anxieties of being an expatriate. The site was named one of the best Japan Blogs on the Web by Tofugu and was spotlighted by The Japan Times.

Eryk has written for *McSweeney's*, *The Japan Times*, *Tofugu* and *Kulturaustausch*. His work as a visual artist has been covered in *The New York Times* and elsewhere.

He currently lives in London.

4116258R00118

Printed in Great Britain
by Amazon.co.uk, Ltd.,
Marston Gate.